SINGING THE LANDSCAPES OF QUEER SELF

Jessye Dylan DeSilva

SINGING THE LANDSCAPES OF QUEER SELF

Gender, Religion, and Community in the Northeastern United States

The Queer and LGBT+ Studies Collection

Collection Editor

Patrick Thomsen

LPp

British Library Cataloguing in Publication Data
A CIP record for this book is available from the British Library.

ISBN: 9781916704015 (pbk)
ISBN: 9781916704039 (ePDF)
ISBN: 9781916704022 (ePUB)

The right of Jessye Dylan DeSilva to be identified as the Author of this work has been asserted by them in accordance with the Copyright, Design and Patents Act 1988.

Cover design by Fiachra McCarthy
Book design by Rachel Trolove of Twin Trail Design
Typeset by Newgen Publishing, UK

Lived Places Publishing
P.O. Box 1845
47 Echo Avenue
Miller Place, NY 11764

www.livedplacespublishing.com

Abstract

Singer songwriter and music professor Jessye Dylan DeSilva (she/her/hers) narrates a collection of stories that guide the reader through her journey, growing up in suburban and rural northeastern settings, as the child of a Baptist minister. Jessye's beginnings in a conservative religious household would come to inform her growth as she navigated adolescence and adulthood as a queer person, poet, musician, academic, and spiritual agnostic. Traversing religious trauma, eating disorders and body dysmorphia, queer friendship and loss, and a mid-life return to the music industry, Jessye uses recollection, song lyrics, and storytelling to examine the intersections of place, queer identity, and embodiment in the late twentieth and early twenty-first century United States.

Key words

Autobiography, gender, lived experience, music, popular culture, LGBTQIA2S+, religious trauma, identity, memoir, queer adolescence, queer childhood, queer family

Content warning

This book contains references to subjects and situations that may cause distress to some readers. This includes references to:

- Homophobia
- Transphobia
- Religious trauma
- Eating disorders
- Sexual Assault
- Addiction
- Suicide

Contents

Prologue

As I write this, I'm sitting in a beautiful co-working space over-looking Boston Harbor. The sea has been both a source of disquieting fear and quieting peace throughout my life. As I stare at the undulating waves, I'm struck by two memories: one is of my father holding four-year-old me tightly in the water as throat-tearing screams rise from deep within my little body. In the other, I am sitting by the ocean as a teenager with a sketchbook, only months after coming out as gay to my parents, plumbing the depths of my adolescent fears and heartbreak and furiously scratching it all onto the page.

Today, only days after beginning gender-affirming hormone replacement therapy (HRT), I've decided to leave my apartment in an outfit that brings me a modest sense of gender euphoria. I've opted for a long, black sweater dress, western boots, layered turquoise necklaces, black lipstick, and a sensible wing of liner at my eyes – I'm calling this look "Goth Bea Arthur." It feels right that I took this slightly scary step to come to a mostly empty public place, and curl myself into a quiet little nook with a big window to silently plug away at my writing.

Growing up on the northeastern side of the United States in the late 1980s and 1990s, "the shore," was my family's summer vacation destination of choice. As such, I've been privileged to develop a cordially affectionate relationship with the sea. The first nine years of my life were spent in the southwestern suburbs of Philadelphia, Pennsylvania, so my oceanside visits were relegated to a week or two every year – I wouldn't say we were close, but each time we caught up it was as if I'd never left. For as long as I can remember, the sea has held a sense of reverence and awe-inducing fear, and yet, to sit by the ocean, or to cool my feet in its shallows has always brought me closer to myself. I still feel the most comforting spiritual nakedness when I spend time with the sea.

I was born on March 12, 1983, in a little first floor room in Mercy Fitzgerald Hospital in Yeadon, Pennsylvania. I'm a Pisces sun with my moon in Aquarius and Aries ascendant if you care about that sort of thing. At the time of my birth, my mother was working as a secretary at a small law firm and my father was attending a local conservative Protestant seminary, studying to become a preacher. I spent the first few years of my life with my parents in the attic apartment of my father's stony old childhood home, where my grandmother still lived at the time. For the first nine years of my life, my parents did not stray more than an hour from their family homes, but eventually, the calling of the ministry "led" my father to rural New Hampshire, and then eventually to southern New Jersey.

Along the way I've been many things. I have been a Christian. I have been a preacher's son. I have been a heretic. I have been and still am a white person. I have been a gay teenager in dark eyeliner, dabbling in witchcraft. I have been an opera singer, a nonbinary person, an atheist, an agnostic, a songwriter, and a trans woman. These are a handful of the identities that intersect and collide to inform my experience as a human on planet Earth.

What follows is a glimpse of my story through washes of memory and song lyrics I've penned along the way.

Unceded ancestral, traditional, and contemporary
lands of the Massachusett tribal nation
Boston, Massachusetts, USA
August 31, 2024

Learning objectives

- Discuss how societal and religious expectations around gender and sexuality affect the development of queer and transgender identities, using specific examples from the author's experiences.

- Describe how chosen family and queer community provide support and resilience in the face of discrimination and rejection.

- Articulate how popular culture, music, and media representation function as sources of inspiration for queer identity formation.

- Compare and contrast the author's experiences of coming out as gay and trans from the 1990s to the present with other popular representations and published memoirs.

- Appreciate the effects of religious trauma on LGBTQ+ youth and explore how arts-based practices can offer healing experiences.

1
Queen of the backyard

Queen of the backyard

Tripping over tree trunks, running through the weeds
Dandelions sing to the faeries in the willow trees.
Barefoot in the backyard, ruling like a Queen
Holding court with the clover and the summer
*   breeze.*

Travel the world in the space of a day.
Music is a sound, not an inkblot on a printed page.
A stick is a wand and a blanket is a cape.
Weird is just a word, not a thing that brings you
*   shame.*

Chorus:
Mighty is your joy, mighty is your joy
Blissful unaware of the growing pain stings
Little girl-boy, little girl-boy
Singing to the witch in the piano strings.

Revel in the joy of the mid-day things.
Caterpillar spells turn to butterfly wings.

Back when the world was all sticky and sweet,
The day was like a table, laid for you to eat.

Way back then your favorite color was green.
Just a pixelated world through the lens of an old
    porch screen,
With front row seats to the thunder and the rain
Back before you knew anything about pain.

(Chorus)

I'm coming back for you.
I'm coming back for you.
I'm coming back for you.
I'm coming back for you.

I never really needed an invisible friend.
Scratches and scrapes, my mother's kisses could
    mend.
Fumbling with flowers and singing to the stones
With nobody around to make me feel alone.

(Chorus)

Keep singing to the witch in the piano strings.
Keep singing to the witch in the piano strings.

By the mid-1980s, my father had accepted a position as the preacher at East Goshen Bible Church – a conservative, non-denominational, fundamentalist Protestant church in the suburbs of Chester County, Pennsylvania. As part of the position, our family would live for free in the parsonage – a modest, four-bedroom house, situated just across a large corn field from the church itself. When we moved there, the house was surrounded on three sides by expansive fields. There was a nice cluster of old oak trees to shade the home, and an old, weathered picnic table just outside the kitchen window in the back yard. For the first four years or so of my life, these were the borders of my world.

I have a smattering of gauzy memories from my early childhood, no doubt supplemented by old photos, home movies, and hallowed family lore. I am told that I was a precocious child. Growing up, my parents often spoke of how advanced I was – speaking and singing from infancy, drawing realistic human figures at an early age, and developing an impressive vocabulary for a toddler. While one might think that this sort of reinforcement would lead to a healthy self- image, I can assure you that it did not. Rather, there was such an overwhelming expectation and I was often chastised for "childish" behavior when I was, in fact, only a child. I was the firstborn – a title that carries a whole host of familial expectations – and my parents were simply doing their best to raise their first child. I was such an odd child that, at times, they simply didn't know what to do with me or how to address the things that came out of my mouth.

Three of my earliest memories took place among the trees surrounding my childhood home. These memories have done a great deal in shaping my sense of self, and also involve incidents for which I was chastised or at least, gently corrected for my behavior. I'm no psychologist, but I think young children are often taught first how **not** to behave.

When I was very young, I was fascinated by what I perceived as the traits and signifiers of femininity. These (white, cis) feminine signifiers are clearly identifiable in many of the drawings my parents have saved from my preschool years – princesses and fashion models, wearing high- heeled shoes, luxurious gowns with cinched waists, and long, flowing hair.

My father – who was himself an art school dropout prior to attending seminary – was conflicted. He was proud of my seemingly innate artistic ability, but concerned by my preoccupation with femininity. One day, while my mother stood at the kitchen window, she overheard a tiny voice speaking and singing like a 1930s Disney princess. She looked down at the old picnic table and saw me, holding fists of wilted weeds and grass, talking to them like dolls. I was so fascinated by the idea of long hair and the way it moved that I had purposely allowed the plants to wilt in the warmth of my little hands, so they looked and moved like long locks of hair. At first, my parents were amused and charmed by my little plant people. Whenever they took me to a restaurant, all they needed to do to keep me occupied and quiet was to give me the parsley garnish from their plates. When they realized that my "plant people" were actually "plant dolls," it became a problem.

In the short time we had lived in the neighborhood, we had been introduced to some of the neighbors. Although they weren't church-going folk, my parents thought it would be good for me to meet the little boy who lived down the street. His name was Kenny. We were the same age, and I suppose he was mostly interested in the "right things" for a boy: video games, sports, etc.

We would often get together and play *Teenage Mutant Ninja Turtles* on his new Nintendo console and while I wasn't particularly interested in TMNT myself, I loved watching the movement and colors of the pixelated images.

One day while we were playing video games in Kenny's basement, he told me that he had walked in on his parents having sex and had caught a few glimpses of a pornographic movie they were watching. I had little to no knowledge of human sexuality at this stage, other than knowing that sometimes when I touched myself in bed it felt good and made me sleepy.

Soon enough, Kenny and I began exploring our bodies together, the way kids sometimes do, and this soon became a bit of a ritual and much of the focus of our time together. One day, while we were playing in the tall grass by his house, we hadn't heard his mother approaching. She was clearly alarmed and stammered until she managed to tell us to go inside. This, of course, led to her calling my parents and me being sent home.

I don't remember what was said when my father finally came to speak to me in my bedroom, but the moments spent waiting for him felt excruciatingly long. What I do remember about that conversation was the shame. I remember the look of abject terror on his face and the way his voice trembled as he tried to explain to me that what Kenny and I had done was wrong and sinful in God's eyes. Mostly I remember the burning flush of my cheeks and the pit in my stomach, because I knew I wouldn't be able to stop thinking about the things I had done with Kenny, even though it was clear they would never happen again. That was the day I learned to hide and fear my own body. Kenny and I really didn't see much of each other after that.

The third of these "core memories" is from the same period. I feel it's important to clarify that my parents were never violently angry with me in these situations. At the time, they did believe corporal punishment was a valid parenting tool, but it was mostly a threat when I was young. The fear was usually enough to keep me in line. While I don't seem to remember ever being struck myself, I do carry the sense that these conversations were approached with the utmost seriousness. I guess "I'm not mad, I'm disappointed" really stuck with me. Still, if I'm honest, my father seemed more scared than disappointed or angry. My father has always seemed to me a kind and gentle man; cautious and thoughtful before he speaks.

The more time I spend with these memories, the more my father's hesitant approach weighs on me. It was as if he was so afraid of me and what my gender and sexuality might mean that he handled me with protective gloves. There was also a sadness in him I still can't quite define or explain. He wasn't some villainous religious zealot who heartlessly indoctrinated me with harmful ideology and toxic masculinity. He truly believed in the healing power of talking through important conflicts and moreover he often said that he loved me, which is more than many fathers seem able to muster. In many ways, he was as much a fragile and lost soul as I was, himself a victim of the indoctrination of masculine shame. Even from a very young age, I perceived his struggle to truly believe the dogma he recited from the pulpit each Sunday in church.

Study questions

1. How does DeSilva's narration of her early childhood speak to the strangeness of "growing sideways" as described in Kathryn Bond Stockton's *The Queer Child: Or growing sideways in the twentieth century* (2009)?

2
10,000 Things (a letter to my mother)

10,000 Things

When the sound of my disdain's too loud to hear me
and there's clouds of self-destruction in my view
My body feels just like a fleshy coffin holding me
*   inside*
and there's noise in me so thick that I can't breathe.

It's one of 10,000 little things
between myself and me

I catch a glimpse of myself in a storefront walking by
hearing whispers from a shiny piece of glass just
*   telling lies*
I try to quiet all the voices telling me that's all I am
but I'm fixated on the sound of footsteps telling me I
*   can't.*

It's just one of 10,000 little things
between myself and me

Turn up the sound
of music in my bones
and I am found
I've carved myself a home
out of 10,000 little things

One of 10,000 little things
between myself and me.

Most of my earliest memories are more like cinematic flashes of color and place. I suppose I hadn't yet developed much of a sense of proprioception, so it's as if I'm not physically present in these snapshots – or rather, I don't really find myself sucked back into my body as it was then, or any version of my body, really. I'm just an observer.

In one of these vignettes, I see you standing in your old bedroom in our East Goshen house. Everything has that sort of muddy beige color of the late seventies and early eighties – it's almost like my mind puts a "retro" Instagram filter on everything. You are getting ready for another in an endless string of Sunday morning church services. I now have a sense of how young you really were, but in my child-brain you weren't young or old – you were just my mother. I'm likely conflating many memories into one, because I can't get a read on a specific hairstyle or outfit, but I usually see you with a permed, short, mullet-ish haircut, wearing large, round, plastic-framed glasses, and a mid-length, floral 1980s-style prairie dress, with modest shoulder pads and a large, lacy, bib-front neckline. You've stepped into a pair of nude, sensibly heeled shoes. It's all **very** *a la mode* for a conservative preacher's wife circa 1986.

I'm guessing I was about three years old at this point. I loved to draw women in beautiful dresses and pumps as a child. I learned the word "pumps" from a commercial for women's shoes that I probably caught while watching daytime television with you. As a young child, I found myself imagining and illustrating these sorts of "feminine ideals," and although I soon encountered Barbie dolls (in commercials only, of course, as I wasn't permitted to play with them) and Disney princesses, at this age, you were still my model and ideal of what femininity looked like.

You were beautiful. You moved with a gentleness and a consideration of others within your space. You put a great deal of effort into adorning yourself for events like Sunday service, where you knew you'd be perceived by others. You matched your shoes with your purses, and considered what shade of lipstick to pair with your dress. You washed and blew out your hair, and occasionally even set it with the strangely sci-fi looking set of hot rollers that lived on top of the toilet in your bathroom. Most importantly though, you were simply my mother. You were my main source of comfort, protection, nourishment, and love. I would not have known any other way to perceive you than with adoration.

And yet, in this memory, I can see you nervously tugging at your dress. You repeatedly pull and smooth areas in the fabric where you feel it is too tight or too revealing – perhaps it doesn't feel like a sufficient enough coat of armor to shield your softer parts from the eyes of others – or even your own gaze. You shift your weight between each foot, turn in semicircles, and purse your lips as you assess your image in the full-length mirror from various vantage points. You sigh with such heaviness I can almost feel the air tremble around me. In some versions of this memory, I even hear you speak cruelly to your own reflection. "I'm so fat. I have nothing to wear. Nothing looks right on my body."

Eventually, you pull out a tube of soft, rosy fuchsia lipstick – the finishing touch perhaps, but when you apply it, I realize it is less of an accent or decoration, and more of a coat of war paint. If you could smear it all over your face, perhaps you would, and if you could add more layers of loose, camouflaging fabric to your body you might also do so, but this will have to do. Time is running late, and you have to get me dressed and ready because, heaven forbid the preacher's wife be late to Sunday School. Sundays were a marathon of demonstrative piety that began at 9:00 a.m. with Sunday School classes for both adults and children before the main event of Sunday morning service at 11:00 a.m., and didn't end until at least 8:00 p.m. after the evening hymn sing and sermon.

I'm not sure of the developmental psychological machinery behind how we as humans begin to associate memory with the present to make meaning of our lives. For whatever reason, this little nostalgic vignette comes to me often, particularly in moments of self- judgment. I am often struck by this shard of memory when I'm standing in front of my own full-length mirror, getting ready for whatever my own day has in store for me. I'm sure there is something here about how we learn to regard ourselves not just by how our parents treat us directly, but rather by how they treat themselves. We only know what we see – not only in terms of our perception of beauty (of course, the most important person in my young life would be beautiful), but also in terms of how we see our parents interact with their world and themselves.

There is something jarring about having one's perceptions and beliefs shaken and contradicted so firmly, especially when that jolt of dissonance comes from a person you deeply trust. At best, these instances provide a brief moment of instability followed by a sense of nuance or clarity, and at worst they can set off a spiral of self-questioning that rattles our very sense of self. I looked at you, the person I loved more than anything and trusted above all else as the arbiter of knowledge and truth, as a person of utter and absolute beauty. Then, you – whose word I took as gospel truth at the age of three – spoke aloud the words "I am ugly." How could this be? What does this mean? Ugly is bad. Ugly is detestable. Ugly is akin to sinful, isn't it? At least, that was the case in the mind of a toddler, who had learned to see things through binary comparison and contrast. Little ones often learn language through the structure of "this is not that." A boy is not a girl. A cat is not a dog. Bad is not good. Ugly is not beautiful.

If the person I love, rely on, and trust above all else is "ugly," or if her assessment of herself as "fat" takes place within the same context, then that must also mean that "fat" is "ugly," and "ugly" is "bad." What else have I been wrong about? Could my Father also be ugly? Could he be bad too? Am I ugly? Am I fat?

I don't think I had put much thought into my own appearance up until this point, but this experience threw everything into question. Aside from watching you get ready, any time I had walked in on you or Daddy in a state of undress, your instinct was to cover yourselves and rush me out of the room. The message I received was largely that bodies were to be hidden and ashamed of, so I suppose I had very little sense of my own, let alone whether it was attractive or not. I don't believe I could have described my own appearance at this age, but I do know that I had been told on multiple occasions by multiple people how much I resembled my father and mother. So hearing a parent describe themselves as ugly brought a lot into question.

Now, I'm not saying my brain followed these exact lines of thought in that very moment. I honestly don't know. But I am doing a lot of "inner child" work in therapy, so perhaps this is just another self-assigned exercise in empathizing with tiny me. I'm also not recounting any of this to make you feel sad or ashamed or as though you failed at parenting in this one moment which you likely have no memory of. Another thing I'm learning in therapy is that we say and do things every day without attaching much importance to them, while others in our lives – children, especially – often hold onto these moments in big ways. This isn't anyone's "fault," it's just how brains develop, or so I've been told.

We both know that "self-image" and "self-worth" are really complex things , shaped by experience. Our experience is constantly colored and influenced not only by our parents, friends, family, and teachers, but also by societal constructs like "gender" and "beauty" that we learn through consumption of popular culture. Sooner or later, those things would have come into my tiny field of vision even if you saw yourself as the most gorgeous gift to humanity. For me, those two particular constructs – gender and beauty – have always been particularly and often troublingly intertwined.

I can't tell you when I first had a sense of my own gender. It's way more complicated than "I always **knew** I was a girl." I didn't. And frankly I think that particular narrative being held up as the dominant one for trans people is reductive and problematic. I knew how I felt from an early age, and I knew that what I was told by others was in stark contrast to my feelings. I always felt that, in some secret space perhaps meant only for me, I was more like the girls I knew than the boys. I also knew that according to prevailing wisdom, I was "a boy." Still, I tried desperately to hold onto whatever vestiges of "femininity" (what even **is** that? Fuck if I know...) I could, whether it was in my own self-expression and embodiment or simply in indulging my artistic eye. At the very least, I could observe and appreciate feminine beauty, and perhaps these crumbs of vicarious joy could be enough to pull me through.

I loved watching you get dressed up. Little children need to experience, imitate and establish a tactile connection with everything, especially the things they admire or enjoy – so of course, I snuck into your closet and clomped around in those sensible nude heels. I got into your makeup case and smeared myself (and sadly, the walls of our home) in that rosy lipstick. I don't know that **that** was the moment "I knew" I was trans. Lots of children of all genders do this.

What I do know is that that memory is also pivotal and lingering.

Much like I was in the memory of you getting ready for church, I was jolted from a moment of exploration and joy, into the stinging knowledge that things like makeup and high heeled shoes were not for me. These things were wrong for little boys. I thought

I knew how I felt, who I was, what felt good, what felt right. But I guess I didn't because my Mom and Dad said I was wrong. The Bible said I was wrong – I couldn't read it myself, but that's what everyone told me. My god, even television told me I was wrong. I didn't see a lot of people there whose experiences mirrored mine, but when I did, they were being gawked at like circus animals while studio audiences groaned and made sounds of disapproval, shifting uncomfortably in their seats. I remember RuPaul on *Geraldo*, the daytime talk show. I remember trans women and drag queens competing in cruel "beauty pageants" with cis women on *Maury Povich*. I remember "that's a **man**, Maury."

I suppose I never really learned how to trust myself. I started looking at my body as though I wasn't sure if my eyes were playing tricks on me. I saw what was there, but also, I saw what I imagined others might see. I started to see you with your eyes, and maybe with society's eyes. I think it was still easier for me to cut through the bullshit and see **you**, as well as others, with eyes of love. I still did and have always thought you were beautiful, but for some reason I was never quite sure who or what was staring back at me in the mirror. I started to internalize those commercials I watched with Barbie dolls and impossibly thin, polished, white cis women, and so in my imaginary world I formed some sort of "me" who looked like them.

Every time I glanced in the mirror or felt someone else's eyes on me, though, I experienced that electric jolt of "reality" being forced upon me.

This feeling of dissonance bled not only into my perception of my gender, but also of my own body size, shape, and worth.

I had so thoroughly imprinted an idealized image of thinness onto myself that when I looked in the mirror or tugged at any tiny ounce of fat on my belly, I wasn't sure what I was seeing or feeling. Eventually I began to magnify everything and assume that **my** perception couldn't be trusted. I'm still never quite sure if I've got distorting glasses on or if I'm looking through a funhouse mirror when I see myself in photos or reflective surfaces. If what I see differs in any way from what I have been taught is beautiful then I **must** be fat, and since I had learned that fat was ugly and bad, I must be those things too.

And so the cycle goes. We do the best we can with what we know and have access to. That is no small thing, particularly in the scope of all the world throws at us. I just want you to know that I still see you with those untainted, toddler's eyes. I still *know* that you are beautiful.

My song, "10,000 Things" is about the ways that body dysmorphia, gender dysphoria, and so many other things disconnect me from my own body and distort my sense of self. It's about that jolt of realization when I gaze into any reflective surface and see not so much my own view, but the projected view of what I fear others might see. My solution for much of my life has been to retreat inward – to go so deeply into myself, my intellect, my dream world – that I dissociate from my own body. And yet wherever I go, there I still am.

I'm still trying – and getting better, I should say – at reigniting that childlike idea of what beauty means. Our bodies hold so much. Your body cocooned me for nine months, nourishing the cells and tissue that would become me and creating the environment in which they could grow. After I emerged, that same body laboured to care for and protect me. It held and comforted me in times of distress and joy. Your body has encased the spirit of a person I love and admire so deeply all these years later. What is all this if it is not beautiful?

My body is capable of making the music and poetry that sustain me in times of pain and empower me in times of joy. My hands pen words of power and human connection. They move keys on an instrument whose soundboard has sent shudders of amazement through my very soul since I first heard you play it years ago. The muscles in my belly and back power the bellows of my lungs, creating sounds that rattle the rafters, and my bones ring with the resonance of my sorrows and my successes.

> "Turn up the sound of music in my bones, and I am found.
> I've carved myself a home out of 10,000 little things."

Study questions

1. DeSilva describes a childhood moment of gender transgression and the realization that makeup and heels "were not for me" according to societal and familial norms. How might Judith Butler's concept of the "heterosexual matrix" – the grid of cultural intelligibility through which bodies, genders, and desires are naturalized – help us understand this formative experience of being policed into the category of maleness and masculinity?

2. The final paragraphs affirm the inherent beauty and worth of all bodies, with their capacity to cocoon, create, heal and resound. How does DeSilva deploy poetic and musical

language to subvert dominant scripts about which bodies are valued? What is the significance of this rhetorically and politically in the context of trans liberation?

3.   DeSilva interrupts the dominant narrative that trans people "always knew" their gender identity from a young age, finding it reductive. In what ways does this piece offer a nuanced narrative of trans identity development as expressed?

3
Firecracker

Firecracker

I used to stomp around wearing my mother's
high-heeled shoes
Smudge myself in war paint, fuchsia pink
I learned to strike 'em down with something quiet and
intense
Now tell me little boy, what can you do?

I'm not a pansy
I am no shrinking violet
I will not pander to the whims of your disdain
All of your anger
and all your self-loathing rage
cannot withstand the multitudes that I contain

Chorus:
Come at me with your anger
Come at me with your slander
'cuz I'm a little firecracker
and I'll be standing when your rage crumbles to dust.

There's just a razor line from fascination to disgust
and words like poisoned arrows find their mark.

Before you learned to kill the things the world won't
    let you have,
Where was the part of you you used to trust?

I'm not a pansy
I am no shrinking violet
I will not pander to the whims of your disdain.
All of your anger
And all your self-loathing rage
Cannot withstand the multitudes that I contain

(Chorus)

I can be a sort of a flight risk
A bit of a spender with my trust
But I'm a symphony of color, sound, and light
A little too sentimental
A bleeding heart if you must
But if you cross me I am not above a fight.

(Chorus)

I can't pinpoint the precise origin of my lifelong fascination with witches. My earliest encounters with magical, wicked women were likely through animated Disney films like *Snow White* and *The Little Mermaid*. I have faint memories of pretending to be the old, haggard, apple- peddling queen in disguise while playing outside in my childhood playhouse. Not long after, my parents rented *The Little Mermaid* for me on VHS cassette and I voraciously watched it over and over until it needed to be returned – I even recall my impatience as I waited, fidgeting, for the machine to rewind the tape for me to watch it again. While the character of Ariel has been one of my favorites since childhood, it was her nemesis Ursula, her alter ego Vanessa, and similarly the Evil Queen in *Snow White* who captured my childhood fascination.

It would be easy to turn this chapter into an essay on nerd culture and queerness – indeed, my childhood love of witches would soon lead to a predilection for all things spooky and paranormal, which would eventually intersect with comic book superheros and an encyclopedic knowledge of a particular rock 'n' roll high priestess (more on these later). However, I see a through-line here that has less to do with fantasy and nerd culture and more to do with a depiction of embodied and symbolic femininity I've craved all my life.

I was raised in a socioreligious culture that not only demonized overt sexuality, but also upheld the cisheteronormative male ideal as the center of all that was good and true. Women were to be subservient to their husbands – even "The Virgin" Mary herself was quoted as saying "I am but the handmaiden of the Lord". I was taught by both the church and society that women and girls were weaker, more fragile creatures than their male counterparts. The 1980s and early 1990s were also a time of intense cultural fear of the threat of Satanism in the United States and thus, in the small religious bubble inhabited by my family, anything mystical or spiritual that was not Christian was deemed demonic.

And so, my backyard play of cackling witches and magic spells was doubly troubling for my father. There was of course, the "black magic" of it all, but then there was also the cross- gender play. In retrospect, I find it telling that the fairytale witches

I became most fascinated with were those who used their powers for physical transformation. Snow White's stepmother transformed herself into a supposedly unthreatening (although, I always found her quite creepy) old woman, and the sea witch Ursula transformed herself into a gorgeous femme fatale rival for the prince's affections. Another favorite (albeit somewhat less fabulous) was Madam Mim of *The Sword in the Stone*, whose transformative powers extended to the animal realm. My inner armchair psychologist is more than a little aware of the trans subtext in these characters for a young trans child.

I don't think the idea of a trans child was even on the radar of my white, conservative parents in the 1980s. At the time, prevailing popular culture was preoccupied with the villainization of homosexual men as disease-carrying deviants, and "cross- dressing" was simply seen as a symptom of the illness. To me, trans people simply didn't exist, and so I suppose I identified even more with an exiled, monstrous sea witch in a fairy tale. I soon learned that not only were witches off limits, but fairy tales themselves were less- than-desirable in the pursuit of the illusion of masculinity. After all, where was a strapping young lad supposed to see himself in these tales? Certainly not in the distressed damsel. And the prince was really a stand-in for male desirability from the female gaze, so that was off-limits. Still, I never found myself afraid of the "evil" witches and sorceresses in these tales. More often than not, I found myself rooting for them.

* * *

In the early 1990s, my world revolved around Saturday mornings. Like so many of my generation, I lived for those few precious hours huddled with a bowl of sugary cereal in front of the magical altar of the family television – hours my sisters and I sat, drunk with the power of our temporary claim over the remote control. The focal point of my Saturdays soon became the original *X-Men* animated series.

Here were the familiar "witches" of my past, reflected in characters like the weather goddess Storm, the superhuman Rogue, and the ethereal telepath Jean Grey/Phoenix. And yet, these women fought alongside the men and were considered heroes. Although society marginalized them for their mutations (a queer allegory that has been discussed by many), they were written as the protagonists of their own stories who, rather than waiting for a man to save them, often did the saving themselves. Conveniently, comic book superheroes were "for boys," weren't they? Was this the fantasy world I had been waiting for all along?

Like so many of my fellow elder millennials, the *X-Men* cartoon became a gateway to the rich and epic world of the comic book series for me. Since predominant cultural wisdom relegated superheroes to the world of boys, it was socially acceptable to ask my parents for comic books and action figures without fear of such things marking me as queer. Eventually, I began to save my allowance for the latest issues – requesting action figures and larger , hard cover trade collections of the comics for birthdays and Christmas.

While my male peers obsessed over machismo characters like Wolverine, I devoured the stories of Ororo Munroe/Storm and Jean Grey/Phoenix. The statuesque Ororo was orphaned in Cairo as a child and made her way as a prodigious street thief until her weather-controlling powers manifested in adolescence, at which point she was worshipped as a goddess. In my opinion, Storm has always been the most fashionable of the *X-Men* – with costumes that evolved with the fashions of the day. In her earliest appearances, Storm wore her white hair long and free-flowing, with a crown-like headpiece, tall boots, and flowing, robe-like capes. She was depicted in the early years as a sort of "earth mother" prototype – emotionally and spiritually in tune with the world around her, with a nurturing and warm rapport with her teammates. There is much about the early depictions of Storm that embrace "high femme," and yet, it is often remarked upon in the comics that she is one of the most powerful mutants on Earth – surpassing most of her male counterparts.

In the mid-1980s, Storm entered a punk, almost butch phase – getting in touch with her darker, edgier side and donning a mohawk, studded collar, distressed jeans, and a leather vest. During this period, she was even stripped of her powers for a number of years, forcing her to further reckon with who she was as a woman, apart from the mutant powers that had defined her until then. One might think that in a superhero comic about superhuman beings, a character stripped of their powers would be relegated to a backseat role, but no! Storm was such a strong and capable human that she was promoted to team leader of the X-Men, even without her abilities! This is my personal favorite era of Storm in the X-Men comics. As a kid, I thought superficially that her punk rock styling was just visually cool, but in subsequent reflections, I really believe it was here that I saw a woman evolving, exploring a gender presentation that embraced the masculine, leading a mixed-gender team into battle, all while reckoning with her sense of self. I had never seen a woman like this in popular media – certainly not in the Bible stories I had been fed since birth! – and I've never looked back.

Phoenix's story is one that has stuck with me through the years. The character of Jean Grey was one of the first class of X-Men in the 1960s "Silver Age," at a time when women in comics were portrayed as little more than "the girl." Early Jean Grey (whose code name at the time was Marvel Girl) was a telekinetic who could move objects with her mind, and whose powers eventually evolved to include telepathy. Beyond her powers she was often treated as an accessory to the men on her team, frequently caught in a will-they-or-won't-they love triangle with Cyclops and Angel, with her career goals being "to become a fashion model." However, in the mid-1970s, following a plane crash in which she sacrificed her life to save her entire team, Jean was "reborn," as the manifestation of a cosmic force called The Phoenix. Jean as Phoenix is astoundingly powerful in a way that surpasses any known mutant. Aesthetically, she eschews her "mod" 60s mini-skirted uniform for a sleek green leotard with long gold gloves and boots, with the symbol of a phoenix emblazoned on her chest. While her teammates, and the men in particular, are uneasy with the scope of her power and even visibly afraid of it, Phoenix revels in it. Time and again, Phoenix expresses unbridled joy in the use of her cosmic powers, until she eventually goes "dark" (she eats a star!) and must be stopped in order to save the universe.

As an adult, I find myself heavily rolling my eyes at the plot device that suddenly strips Phoenix of agency over her powers and necessitates her being controlled. She is even depicted visually as a more dangerous version of herself – her green costume switching to dark crimson, her pupils whited out, and her hair suddenly longer and wildly curled. The "Dark Phoenix Saga" is incredibly well-written, but I still grieve the loss of this ethereal, ferocious, cosmic force. As a child, when I first read this series, I found myself slowing down and savoring it – knowing that the resolution was coming, but wishing I could somehow manipulate the plot so Phoenix could live. I **loved** her that way. Why is it that male characters are able to teeter on the edge of darkness and struggle with their own duality, while she was suddenly transformed from a powerful person into an "issue" that must be dealt with? And why, oh why, asks this curly gal, must all of the "good girls" have perfectly blown out and straightened locks?

It wasn't long before my father became wary of the "sinful dangers" of comic books. I can recall a book he had in his church study on the "contemporary dangers" facing the youth of the 1990s, in which a picture appeared of Madeline Pryor (The Goblin Queen in the *X-Men* universe) in her gravity-defying, almost full-breast-baring black costume. The picture appeared in a chapter titled "Sex and Sorcery: The Incredible Comic Book Horror Show" with a caption that made note not only of the character's scantily clad appearance, but also of the baby she was offering as a sacrifice (Marrs, T. 1989). While this period didn't permanently end my relationship with Phoenix, Storm, and the *X-Men*, for the time being, I was limited to the problematic gender dynamics of Archie comics (which I read solely for the fashions and fabulousness of Betty and Veronica).

When I was a pre-teen, my parents set up a play date with one of the other boys in the church who was struggling to connect with his peers. While I don't remember much about our time together, what I do recall is connecting more with his young mother, Denise. Denise was a music-lover and had a fantastic new sound system with a CD player. Prior to this point, I'd taken piano lessons and sung hymns in church, but in terms of listening, the cassette tapes of instrumental classical music I fell asleep to at night were about all I'd been exposed to. One day, Denise introduced me to the music of a popular Christian artist named Amy Grant. That was the day I'd unknowingly begun the time-honored Queer tradition of diva worship.

By the mid-1980s, Amy Grant had become the closest thing the Christian music industry had to a full-fledged pop star. Here was a fresh-faced, normatively beautiful, young white girl with a winning smile who wrote love songs to Jesus with a contemporary pop-rock sensibility. Grant's dusky alto vocals even had a slight note of sexiness to them as she sang out her pop-drenched hooks. Soon enough, I began collecting her discography on cassette tape as well as learning to play her songs on the piano. It was the influence of this music that inspired me to become more focused on singing and accompanying myself on the piano during Sunday services.

One year for Christmas, my father and I even used the church sound system to record an "album" of Amy Grant's songs as a gift for the extended family.

While 1980s Christian icons like Amy Grant and Sandi Patty seem about as safe as I can imagine these days, I learned from a gentleman at my father's church at the time that these two were considered by many to be wayward, wanton women. Once, following a Sunday service where I'd performed Grant's "Thy Word," the music leader Dennis took it upon himself to inform my father that Amy Grant was actually divorced, and had even crossed over into mainstream "secular" pop music. While Sandi Patty – another Christian superstar – was also a divorced woman, she had at least continued to dedicate her musical talent "to the Lord," so I suppose she at least had that going for her. While my parents didn't seem too concerned by this revelation, I have to laugh at the realization that even my Christian "diva" was an example of a rebellious, self-empowered woman.

As I approached adolescence, I began to more fully embrace the power of music as a safe outlet through which I could dream and live my inner life. Where I initially began singing exclusively in church, I eventually began performing in school talent shows and spending increasing hours at the family piano in our home. Even in a religious setting, singing was a way to explore my gender somewhat safely. I had little interest in learning songs sung by male artists, preferring rather to sing the sly, sultry religious tunes of Amy Grant in my yet unchanged prepubescent voice. When I sang, the voice that played in my mind was hers, and I learned every quiver of her vibrato, every small riff, and vowel pronunciation. Singing was then, and continued to be a secret world where I could emulate the feminine. So long as I was singing to or about Jesus in church, no one questioned it. I could engage in the musical and the artistic, and all anyone seemed to think was how very admirable it was for "the pastor's son" to use "his" gift for the Lord.

Interestingly, Amy Grant's foray into secular music seemed to offer me my own gateway into the same. My parents didn't seem to mind that I listened to her pop songs, and during this time, they also began to rediscover connections with the non-religious music of their youth. I've mentioned elsewhere that my father never seemed fully at-home with the fundamentalist Christian dogma he was preaching at church. He'd been indoctrinated in seminary and was serving in conservative churches, but it seemed – even then – to be a costume he donned for work. Soon enough, our car rides were serenaded by artists like Crosby Stills Nash & Young, Carly Simon, and Creedence Clearwater Revival on the local Classic Rock radio station, and when the family acquired our first CD player for the stereo system, theirs were some of the first discs to be purchased. Although I lived many years prior without this particular soundtrack to my life, I still think of these as the musicians who raised me.

Somewhere in the liminal space between middle school and high school, a friend introduced me to the music of Fleetwood Mac. Even before the band made their late-1990s comeback, I found myself immediately smitten with the witchy poeticism and rock 'n' roll sensibility of Stevie Nicks. As I mentioned earlier, I've never really tired of the archetype of the witch, and here was a woman who embraced and played with this imagery not only in her music, but also in the way she dressed and styled herself onstage. Of course, during the height of the Satanic Panic in the 1980s, she denied that she was a practicing witch, but as a fan, I felt like I was in on the secret. Even if she didn't burn offerings at a pagan altar in her home, the worlds she wove with her music felt like magic to me and twirling along to her CDs in my bedroom felt like a ritual.

I could probably write an entire book on the impact Stevie Nicks has had on my own gender identity, but suffice it to say, I found in her artistry much of what I'd found in the fairy tale witches and comic book superheroines of my youth. At a time when women in rock music had to prove they were "one of the boys," cropping their hair and donning leather jackets, tight blue jeans, and other androgynous fashions, Stevie leaned into her mystical, Pre-Raphaelite high-femme aesthetic. Everything she wore draped and flowed. She wore her hair long and wild, and donned velvet and silk, twirling like a ballerina to the driving rhythm of her band. And yet, she was still a self-proclaimed rock 'n roller. Whereas this sort of high femme theatricality was often relegated to soft pop music, she insisted upon the legitimacy of her place in the rock 'n roll pantheon, and wailed along ferociously to the screaming guitars of Lindsay Buckingham. She delighted in all things feminine and beautiful, yet she embraced an untamed style of stage performance, influenced heavily by having seen Janis Joplin perform years earlier. She tried to put words to the unseen and the mystical, often taking songs about very tangible real-life love affairs to esoteric and almost indecipherable places. Her lyrics often switched between first and third tenses, creating a sense of mythos around her own life experiences. She wore her heartbreak on her sleeve but insisted that it made her stronger.

In terms of her cultural impact, she went from "the girlfriend" of the guitar prodigy that the band **really** wanted to hire – and given only a couple of songs on the early records – to **the** star of the band who girls and gays would cosplay as at concerts, and eventually at the yearly drag festival "The Night of a Thousand Stevies." Much like Storm, the "girl" X-Man of the 1970s, who would eventually eclipse the most capable of men around her and rise to team leader in the 1980s, Stevie's star power out-shone her former boyfriend's as she became "the main event" of Fleetwood Mac.

Study questions

1. How does Alexander Doty's concept of "queer reading practices" in *Making Things Perfectly Queer: Interpreting Mass Culture* (1993) help us understand how DeSilva recuperates the symbolic function of witches, X-women, and singers in her own gendered self-fashioning?

4
Sundays (a letter to my father)

Sundays

My father's face looked different on Sundays.
Religion was the job he'd settled for.
I'd dress up for the lion's den
In pleated pants and squeaky shoes.
My mother's jaw would set itself for war.

I tried to blend into the old piano,
Pedals barely reached with tiny shoes.
Praying for the blood to douse
The flames of secret sin
Musty rugs and dusty wooden pews.

Chorus:
Burning bushes, weeping stones.
I never felt so all alone.
Sitting timid as a mouse,
A guest in God almighty's house.
If I was good enough for Heaven
Maybe this might feel like home.

My faith felt like a thing with scars and
     bulletholes
And fellowship meant being on display.
Resent and indignation
Served with iced tea and baked beans,
Smiles laced with bitterness and shame.

Now the Father's house, I'm told has many rooms
But no one likes to talk about the fee.
Accommodations don't quite match
The cost of room and board,
For good old fashioned sinners just like me.

There is a fountain filled with blood
Drawn from Emmanuel's veins.
And folks who bathe beneath that flood
Get stuck with guilt and shame.

(Chorus)

Now I've learned to try to see myself unclouded.
I've lived with scarlet letters on my chest.
Too long a time with pleasure
Came the hot flood of regret.
I've hid between the margins,
Sung hosannas with the rest.
I killed the fatted calf to make amends for what
     I lacked
But truth, I've found's the thing that tastes
     the best.

You always seemed a little different on Sunday mornings. There was a weariness in you, almost as if you had to steel yourself for the day to come. I want you to know that I saw that, and I know that it wasn't 'just easy' for you either.

I remember Mom always telling us to give you space – not just in the morning while you did last-minute prep for your sermon and picked out a suit and tie, but also after the morning service. After all, your day was far from over. You still had youth group and an evening hymn- sing and service to lead, often with visits to the sick and elderly peppered in between. When there was time for a nap, you'd often crash into your bed to nurse one of your frequent migraines.

I guess I'm recounting all of this because now I know that it wasn't just your introverted nature that made these days so long and trying for you. You seemed... different. You sort of became a more stoic, serious version of my father – or perhaps someone who seemed very little like the father I knew at all. As the years went by, it almost felt like this was a role you'd committed to playing long ago, and you just had to resign yourself to it, either until you died or were able to retire.

Mom also seemed different. She was steely and short-tempered. She dutifully applied her makeup and selected a dress I know she'd never wear for any other occasion, and proceeded to tug and pull at her clothing while she made self-deprecating remarks about her weight. During the service, she'd often glare at us from the choir loft just off to the side of the pulpit. Her attention seemed as though it might be anywhere but on "worship." She didn't really choose to be a pastor's wife, but she'd chosen you.

I don't know that she truly felt regret or bitterness about that, but I never got the impression that the role of "pastor's wife" was one she really wanted.

It can at times be easy for me to settle into the narrative that weekly church services were harder on me, the queer child, than the rest of the family. It would be all too convenient to focus on my own alienation in this space, and while I do reckon with that, I also understand now that in some ways you both also felt cut off, judged, obligated, or even "stuck" in that life. For all the pretense of welcome and unconditional love and community, the religious spaces we inhabited for most of my childhood were anything but.

There is an old photograph of me, perhaps around the age of four or five. It looks like it was taken in the East Goshen, PA church, perhaps on Easter Sunday. I am dressed in a tiny shirt and tie, with a blue blazer, but I'm also clutching someone's purse and have put on a pair of lacy white gloves that are too big for me, and a white, lacy hat. I am beaming brightly into the camera. I have no memory of the actual context of this photo, but I think of it often, as the joy on my tiny face is in such stark contrast to my actual memories of Sundays at church.

Whose lacy accessories was I wearing? Who took the photo? Was it you or Mom? It must have been taken in jest, but I'm still surprised that it was taken at all, and that I wasn't immediately told by some nervous, embarrassed adult to take these things off. Was this before I was caught in Mom's closet, stumbling around in her high heeled shoes? Was it before I'd been caught with the neighbor's son, "playing doctor"?

I was always a child who wanted to please my parents and authority figures. You've often told me, "What a good baby" I was, but something clicked at some point in early childhood when I began receiving messaging that I was in some way "wrong." Not only did I learn to put aside things that made me feel good, like crushes on boys and playing with dolls and dresses, but I also happily learned to play the role of the good Christian "son." I wore my boy drag each Sunday: shiny, blister-inducing penny loafers that refused to bend when I walked, well-ironed dress slacks, shirts with collars and clip-on ties that made me feel like I was choking. I certainly didn't like the way I looked or felt in these clothes, but everyone made such a fuss and called me "hand-some." When I began to discover an inclination toward music, I sang solos and played piano as often as I could in church. Finally, I found an identity where my "creativity" and "sensitivity" were deemed acceptable forms of "service to the Lord."

The truth is, I didn't really like all of the attention being shone on me. It felt like each time we walked through those heavy church doors a blazing spotlight was shining on everything I tried so desperately to hide. I could feel people's eyes burning holes into the costume I wore at church. I even felt like the eyes of the burly white Jesus portraits were following me. I believed in him then, so of course I knew that "He was always watching," and I could only hope that singing and playing for him was penance enough to make up for the parts of me that were dirty and unacceptable in his sight. Still, I internalized that fear of actually being **seen**. So, in some ways, while music made me feel more myself than any-thing, the added attention felt a bit like scrutiny, and anything positive about it always seemed tenuous at best.

People always talk about "protecting the children" from the influ-ence of queer and trans people. Now they talk about "groom-ing," but then it was less about predatory gay boogie men and more about shielding children from the dark influence of Satan himself. Truthfully, in the mid-eighties and early nineties, I can recall less than a handful of times that I saw or heard of anyone from the LGBTQ+ community. And yet, I can clearly recall those rare instances, because as a child, I always picked up on not only what was said but what was unsaid as well. Children zero in on the ways adults demonize folks who might be like them. In some ways, I learned more about "perversion" from the authority fig-ures who claimed to protect me from such things.

One of the things I've always found curious was your desire for me to sit through the entirety of the church service from a very young age. There was nursery for children who were too young to sit quiet and still during the headier parts of the church ser-vice, but perhaps because I was "so well-behaved, and so smart for my age", you believed that I should try to follow along and learn whatever I could. During our time in East Goshen, aside from schoolyard jeers and the occasional episode of the Phil Donahue daytime talk show which may have featured someone queer, the only other time I remember hearing about homosex-uality was in an evening Bible study series you gave at church. That series on "contemporary issues" also spoke about abortion, "cults," and "devil worship" the latter two of which I remember being quite frightening for a young kid like me. Aside from that, it was more about the things you didn't say or the things you not-so-subtly tried to shield me from. But it's still interesting that you **didn't** choose to censor this particular Bible study from me.

I wonder if that was in any way intentional. Were you afraid that perhaps it was a message I might benefit from hearing? Parents seem to spend a great deal of time and energy worrying over what to shield their children from, and yet those same children hear and see so much that sticks with them and informs the ways they grow.

* * *

I still remember the musty smell of the carpet that cocooned every square inch of the church in Franklin, New Hampshire, where we had relocated in early 1993. It was this strange bouquet of dust, mildew, old wood paneling, and cleaning solution. It smelled of fear, with something shameful and decaying just underneath. Thinking about it now stirs up a lightheaded nausea because the memory is so strong and specific. I can even recall the difference in smell when the sanctuary was being heated for winter, slightly warmer, woodsier, but still with that underlying rot. It was an old building, kept up as well as its small, far-from-wealthy congregation could manage through tithing of their coins and their labor. But I think that smell I remember might be something less tangible than just dust or mold or mice in the walls.

I think I told you about the time Andrés and I drove past the old parsonage in Franklin a couple of years ago. It was in the autumn of 2020, when everyone seemed to be squeezing in their last bits of travel mid-pandemic, before the colder weather forced us all indoors again, providing the perfect incubator for another surge of COVID 19. It was the first time we'd driven through New Hampshire since we relocated to Boston in 2018 for Andrés' faculty position, and I found myself drawn to Franklin with a dreadful urge to share some of my formative years with my partner.

It's strange how flashes of our years in New Hampshire come so quickly and clearly to me in sounds and smells, yet the narrative thread of memory feels so patchy and disjointed. I find myself able to recall earlier memories much more easily, while most of what seems available from these years are emotions, moods, and a more ethereal sense of time and place. Most of what I see when I try to remember this time is cast in a sickly, greenish light, with that stomach-roiling scent attached like "smell-o-vision." Everywhere I turn there's a sense of imminent danger and hyper vigilance. Most of the adult church members I remember give me an inarticulable feeling of unease.

Those years spent in New Hampshire include many firsts: the first time I realized we were "poor," when I was teased mercilessly for the thrift store wardrobe I returned to school with in the fall; the first time I complained about the tasteless, puffed rice cereal in the label-less box Mom had brought home from the WIC center, the federally-sponsored service offering supplemental nutrition for low-income women, infants, and children in the United States; the first time I saw the weight of the profession you'd chosen sitting heavily on your chest and sunken deeply into your tired eyes, after you'd returned from an emergency visit to a woman whose husband had been caught molesting their young children; the first time I walked into church invisibly carrying the red-hot shame of my changing, adolescent body; the first time that body betrayed me at Webster Lake as I struggled to avert my eyes from the boys my age, splashing and swimming about, shirtless in the summer warmth.

You were surrounded by and deemed responsible for so much pain and trauma in those years. You took the job of "shepherd-ing" your congregation so literally, in a tiny urban town filled with trauma and lacking in resources. You took on much more than any one person should. You were therapist, social worker, conflict mediator, **and** spiritual leader in a community that creaked and groaned with the weight of its despair. These many roles were not only soul-crushing, but also far above your pay grade in terms of training. I still know only bits and pieces of the things you wit-nessed during those years of your ministry, and even those snip-pets frequently interrupt my sleep. You did all of this for a wage well below the poverty line (albeit in a community where that was the norm). And for what? I know you did it for your faith and for the people, but who was there to look after and protect you?

It's no wonder my sisters and I struggled to sleep at night, fearing our home – our one sanctuary – might be breached by vicious intruders. No wonder we hid between the seats of the old van you drove whenever a stranger glanced our way in a parking lot. Not because you'd exposed us to danger or neglected our safety in any way, but because your own nerves were so raw and exposed at all times. You were worn threadbare, all the while trying your best to make us feel safe and cared for, when at any moment you might receive a phone call, beckoning you to another con-gregational crisis in the middle of the night. Constantly on call. A shepherd holds vigil for his sheep, after all.

I find it curious that within this space – a small, entirely white, low-income, deeply traumatized community – members were overrun with fear at some faceless, Satanic intrusion. This was a community for which so much of the danger and cycles of abuse came from within, and yet, they – **we** – feared danger from beyond. Fear of the other was pervasive, and it was here that you gave the aforementioned Bible study series on "contemporary issues" facing Christians. Our religious community and immediate family withdrew further inward into isolationism and fear, and this was all at a time when I felt more isolated from you and the church than ever before. I'd wager that, albeit for different reasons, you may have felt more alone than ever too.

I recently brought this time up in conversation with my therapist. I was concerned about my own seeming lack of coherent memories from these years, as well as the somatic response I'd had when I first sat down to write about them. A narrative stream of events is easy to put to paper, but blurry flashes of imagery, scents, and general feelings of unease present a bit of a challenge. To further complicate things, I'd begun to feel nauseous after about an hour spent trying to recollect and write about my memories of our time in New Hampshire. I'd worried that perhaps I was unearthing some deeply repressed traumatic event, and that could still be the case. But my therapist had a different perspective on what I **did** remember.

So much of my work in therapy has been about reparenting my inner child and reckoning with developmental trauma – I don't say this to provoke guilt in you for the job you did as a parent. Apparently, this is something we could all stand to explore a bit.

I am firm in my belief that you and Mom did the best you could with what you had at the time. I also think that change happens whether we want it to or not, and we are always forced in a manner of speaking, to grow up before we are ready.

All of this is to say, that those years spent in New Hampshire – for me, between the ages of 9 and 12 – were full of instances where I believe I saw for the first time, that you and Mom were human. Not only that, but you were struggling and did not, contrary to my prior beliefs, have everything under control. The strain of the trauma you endured during that time was such that you were unable to shield your children from bearing witness to it, and that was a deeply unsettling and destabilizing thing for us to witness as kids. Here were the two people in the world who were "supposed to" protect and care for us, and they were clearly struggling to care for themselves and the many people in the church who looked to and relied on them. How terrible to note that these earth-shattering realizations came, for me, also at a time of early adolescent change!

There in the midst of all of this, I huddled, feeling alone and frightened of everything from beyond and within. My body was changing in ways I hadn't been fully prepared to handle, and I was having thoughts and feelings which were completely at odds with what I was being taught in church. I was still very much a child, and yet my body was pushing me into adulthood, and further toward a sense of gender that felt off for me. All the while, I watched quietly as you and Mom struggled financially and emotionally, in the midst of a community of fearfully isolated people.

We really don't talk much about these years in our collective family history. When we left the church in New Hampshire and moved to New Jersey – closer again to the region, culture, and people you knew well, it was almost as if we ran there as fast as we could. There was this sense of packing our things and moving on, never to look back. I think that for a time, I'd internalized this for myself as shame over the changes I'd experienced in those years. Perhaps you felt similarly – ashamed not only that you were unable to be everything for the people there who asked so much of you, but also because you'd gone there in the first place, and brought your family into those tumultuous years.

I don't know that I'm saying you **have** to talk about this to heal. Everyone deals with trauma in their own way, and I wouldn't have you push yourself toward conversations that don't feel safe. I will say this, though: So much during those years was whispered or left unsaid altogether. We try, especially in adulthood, to seem as though we are wholly self-sufficient and equipped to handle anything, and I'm sure that temptation is stronger for folks who are raising children. But I don't think it was the realization that you weren't okay that caused such unease for me or my sisters, so much as the fact that we'd never been shown before that you were also human. That you also had fears and struggles and shame and uncertainty. One of the greatest joys in my adult life has been the journey toward knowing you and Mom more fully as flawed, confused human beings, who are trying just as hard as I am to find their way through life while doing as much good and as little harm as possible.

I'm grateful for the crack in your infallible, heroic "Dad" façade, because it's not only allowed me to see you more fully, but also to feel less alone in my own fragility and uncertainty about life.

Study questions

1. How does DeSilva's relationship with her father complicate the concept of "hegemonic masculinity" as theorized by R.W. Connell in her 1995 book *Masculinities*?

5
Jeannie Frances/ Comrades in arms

Jeannie Frances

Homeroom 1996
I was just the new kid at your school.
Probing adolescent eyes and whispers
Made me feel just like a fool,
But there was you.

With a voice just like a butterfly
And the openness to meet folks where they're at.
Music in your throat
And lines of poetry just sprouting from your hands
Nothing fake and nothing planned.

Chorus:
Oh Jeannie Frances don't you cry
One day your heart will open wide
And those harsh winds will help you fly
And over time you just might find
There's no need to wonder why
Oh Jeannie Frances don't you weep
You have the prettiest of eyes even you don't believe

With a kind of gleam that you just can't see
But you know you're always beautiful to me.

We became fast friends
And soon we shared all of our secret hopes and
     fears.
When ridicule became too much
We'd build each other up and sing through tears
But still I tried hard not to see

You knew things about me
That I couldn't or I wouldn't now myself
When someone you loved needed you
You'd fold your dreams and wishes on the shelf
Rang your kindness like a bell.

(Chorus)

There was a sadness in smile
And some kind of pain behind your eyes.
You tried on every costume
That there ever was to try.
Kept giving love and grace away
In hopes to find a way to love yourself Busy healing
     hearts
But all the while just wishing you were someone else.

(Chorus)

Yes you know you're always beautiful to me.

Toward the end of my family's time in New Hampshire I'd found a stable group of middle school friends. In the midst of it all, I was still floundering in the sea of adolescent uncertainty and the fear of my own burgeoning queerness. The beginning of eighth grade did not feel like an ideal time to uproot and move to a new school.

For reasons that remain unclear to me, my parents decided that we would make the move in mid-September, and so I'd be starting at my new school in Vincentown, New Jersey about a month late. For most of my childhood each school morning had held a sense of panic and fear, even when I'd been settled into a school, and so this delay of the inevitable was both welcome and agonizing. The painful anticipation hit a high point when I found out that my first day would be "picture day."

The minutiae of self-presentation – from hairstyles to clothing and accessories – has always felt acutely important to my sense of self. I've loved the beauty of fashion since I was young enough to recognize it. Fashion is an extension of my identity, or a shorthand to express my mood on any given day. However, I learned early that the things I found beautiful in terms of clothing and adornment were not "for me." Even years later, as a kid in fifth grade in New Hampshire, I'd proudly donned a neon yellow and pink number I'd picked out at a local Goodwill: an oversized, brightly colored t-shirt, and a pair of ornately printed "Hammer pants." What I didn't know was how passé this style was by 1994, and how all it really screamed to my peers was how poor we were. From the sting of that moment, I tried my best to stick to clothes that, if not the height of current fashion, were at least nondescript and less prone to getting me noticed.

That Tuesday morning in October 1996, I picked out a black, long sleeved polo shirt, ill- fitting black jeans, and a pair of unmemorable black boots. The goal was two-pronged: maybe all-black would make me seem mysteriously cool, but mostly I was hoping to blend in to the point of disappearance.

To start our day, we gathered in our homerooms, organized alphabetically by last name for attendance, sat through announcements over the loudspeaker, and stood to recite the "Pledge of Allegiance". This was pretty standard fare, even in my previous school, but the fear that twisted itself tightly in my chest made the whole experience feel as foreign to me as could be. As I walked in, just like in any movie or television show, the room went quiet with whispers and shifty eyes. The teacher was kind enough, as I recall, as she pointed me to a desk about three seats back in the row closest to her desk, just in front of an awkwardly tall girl wearing thick, granny glasses (not ironically like a mid-2000s hipster, but out of necessity, like a poor kid in the mid-1990s), with wavy, auburn hair. Like recognizes like, and I could see that she was likely a bit of a social pariah, based solely on her weight and social class. Children learn so quickly from their parents to be cruel.

Jeannie was instantly friendly and giggly with me in a way that made me a little uncomfortable. I didn't really know what to do with interest from girls. But she also made me feel instantly warm and safe. I felt like maybe she could really see me.

That first school year in New Jersey was filled with Jeannie. She was an avid reader and loved to write poetry, listen to music, and sing. She had the most otherworldly singing voice I'd ever heard;

that still holds true to this day. I have yet to meet someone with that sort of natural mastery over their singing voice and the ability to spin a musical phrase that would melt your heart. We were kindred spirits. We would sing together, and I would accompany her on the piano. She encouraged me to join the chorus; we quickly nabbed multiple solos for the holiday concert. It was Jeannie who introduced me to the music of Tori Amos, Sarah McLachlan, and, most importantly Stevie Nicks. We watched movies like the classically 1990s *Empire Records* at her house, visited the Jersey Shore in the summer, and dreamed together of our future as famous musicians.

Now, the other side of that year was my embarrassment at being her friend. Not long into my first week, a group of popular boys began to talk to me. They didn't like me. They didn't think I was cool. I was a joke to them. I knew this. And yet, the game for them was to cruelly invite me into their clique, all the while winking and nudging each other with every question they asked me. And so, during school hours, I followed this group of cruel boys around like a needy puppy. I sat with them at lunch. They gave me a name that was not my own: Damon. I'm still not in on the joke, but they thought it was hilarious. I knew it wasn't real, but I felt a proximity to "acceptance," and so I answered to this name. I willingly served as the butt of their jokes that entire year. I talked with Jeannie in homeroom, and for the rest of the day I avoided her like the plague, so long as any of these boys were around. After school – when it counted, I thought – it was all Jeannie and our other pair of outcast friends. By this point in my life, as a closeted, queer child in a conservative religious household, I was used to living a double life. What were two more lives added to the pot? I knew Jeannie wasn't ignorant of what was happening, and yet she remained a loyal, patient, and kind friend. I still find the way I treated her really difficult to sit with all these years later. I used her friendship and camaraderie when I needed it, and discarded her – joining in with the crowds who shunned her – when it suited me. It would take until we were both in our 30s for me to acknowledge and take accountability for this.

That summer, between eighth grade and our first year in the huge regional high school, Jeannie and I were inseparable. We even met a couple of girls from a few towns over who were also into music and choir and would be joining us at Lenape High School in the fall. I finally began to feel the freedom of these friendships and the joyful anticipation of fading into a large high school of over 2,500 students, where those cruel middle school boys could just be a blip in the past. Late in the summer, Jeannie came out as bisexual to some mutual friends. When one of our friends intimated to me that Jeannie might be queer, I panicked. This was too close to my own truth. What did Jeannie know about me? What did our friends know that I was not ready to admit to myself?

Once again, I mistreated Jeannie in the way we only hurt those we take for granted. My immediate reaction was one of disgust. "How could she be bi? What a freak. Weren't we outcasts enough already? Why did she have to try so hard to be different? To be interesting?" My feigned vitriol of disgust and fear was nothing more than a smokescreen for my own self-loathing.

The rift between us didn't last long. Again, Jeannie took the hit on the chin. She was hurt and angry, rightly so. At this point we'd not spoken to each other directly about any of this. I knew I'd hurt her. She knew that. I'd also hurt myself. She knew that, too. She always knew – that was what made our friendship feel so dangerous to me. And yet, she waited for me to come to her, which I eventually did. When that happened, I broke down and confessed that I'd spoken out of a place of terror at my own feelings. This was not a surprise to her, but she never took a stance of "I told you so." She just hugged and cried with me, and thus our bond – two outsiders just walking through the world together – crystallized. What a truly pivotal point in both our lives this must have been. Here we were, not merely friends or soulmates, but comrades.

Refugees. Survivors. About to enter the next chapter in our lives together.

Comrades in Arms

Gods of our immortal youth
Climbing trees and seeking truth
Headphone solitude and whispers
Short on patience, tired of waiting

Chorus:
So I scream and set off the alarms
With my comrades in my arms
And we feel like no one has before
Something sacred in the breaking.

We throw our bodies to the roar
On the sticky V.F.W. floor
Squeezing out the last of summer nights
Late day waking, sunscreen daydreams.

(Chorus)

So we scream
And we scream
And we scream…
So we scream
And we scream
And we scream…

(Chorus)

In September 1997, I began the ninth grade at Lenape Regional High School in Medford, NJ. I went from a small junior high school within walking distance of my house, with a little over 100 students in my grade to a large regional high school two towns over, where I'd enter a freshman class of about 500. The change was staggering, especially for an anxious kid like myself who felt safest with routine and familiarity.

And yet, the previous year had been so fraught with my desperate struggle for acceptance from a group of cruel small-town boys, that part of me reveled in the opportunity to create a new persona for myself. Dressing like a preppy teenage boy, with all my polo shirts and surfer chokers made from puka shells and itchy woven hemp, never really suited me, and my curly hair struggled to conform to the center-parted bowl cut that was so *en vogue* at the time. All of the exhausting work I'd done to conform neither made me happy nor earned me any true friends in the small "it crowd" at Southampton Middle School. A bigger crowd meant more room to fade into the background, or perhaps, more opportunity to make a mark. I wasn't quite sure which avenue I preferred.

Where Southampton had been a small, fairly rural community, the other townships that fed into the larger high school were a bit more suburban, with a slightly higher income bracket. My parents said the district was rated extremely well in terms of public education and resources, but what excited me most was the prospect of a well-funded and respected music program.

Lenape High School boasted an award-winning marching band, a jazz band, and three choral groups, all of which regularly sent students to the audition-only All State choir and band programs. At 14 years old, the only bright spot in a long school day was the promise of music- making and the considerable bonus that I could do it for an actual grade. I immediately threw myself into art classes and choir, and when auditions were posted for the school musical, I was on top of those as well.

What felt most rewarding was the opportunity to meet and interact with so many different types of people. The teacher who directed the school musicals was infamous for casting football players and popular kids in the lead roles – something that evoked bitterness in the music and theater nerds like myself. And yet, even this seemed to foster an interesting sense of community between students who otherwise would have been unlikely to interact.

The musical my freshman year was *Damn Yankees,* which I had never heard of. It's a 1950s Faustian tale of baseball and celebrity. The cast was chock-full of high school jocks, and I was an eager member of the ensemble. As someone who at the time identified as a boy, I was to take part in a locker room scene, where I'd appear, with the aforementioned jocks, in my boxer shorts. Onstage. I was mortified and filled with terror. And yet, Chad, the star quarterback at school, who played the lead role of Shoeless Joe in the show, was so kind to me. He and his football bros all brought dumbbells to the chorus room, which served as our "dressing room" during dress rehearsals and performances, and showed me how to do pushups and bicep curls before we all bared our chests onstage. Chad was also dating Cindy, who played the female lead in the show.

Cindy was a member of the choir and soon became one of my good friends, and by extension, popular, star quarterback Chad became a friend too.

My friendship with Jeannie, introduced me to so many different folks as well. Jeannie was a ray of light wherever she went, and in addition to our choir and theatre connections, she soon fell in with the artsy goth kids. Soon enough, Jeannie and I had found our lunch table with bohemian chic Vera, who somehow only ever seemed to take art classes and wore paint spattered jeans every day, Sophie, the gothiest girl who ever lived; and a small clique of other goths who all said they were vampires. Did I know we were at the "freak" table? Of course. Did I care, when surrounded by such an eclectic and friendly group of people? Not one bit.

One of the most formative people in my adolescence was my high school choir teacher, Mr. Schwab. Mr. Schwab was, in appearance, a classic white, middle-aged teacher tall, dressed in a white Oxford shirt and an unremarkable necktie, sporting a mustache (at a time when mustaches were very much **not** on trend). He was not someone I would have looked at and immediately felt safe with. He could have been just another one of the conservative old white guys at my parents' church. And yet he was so much more.

Mr. Schwab was a musician's musician. An extremely skilled jazz composer, pianist, and arranger, it always seemed to me that perhaps teaching was not his number one passion and plan in life. And yet, his love of music was so contagious, and he couldn't help but treat his students as collaborators. Each year, he would put on what he called the "Pops Concert." This was not your run-of-the-mill, open-to-all high school talent show, but rather the Pops Concert was an audition-only variety show, meticulously curated by Mr. Schwab himself, and recorded at as high a quality as the high school sound equipment could make possible. My freshman year, I somehow landed two songs in the Pops Concert: a cover of Fleetwood Mac's "Landslide," and a moody teenage ballad of unrequited love I'd written for the only other gay kid I knew in school called "You Don't Know."

Performing at this school event soon earned me the respect of a lot of kids I didn't otherwise interact with. I became "that kid who sings really well," and in spite of my own burgeoning queerness, and my general teenage awkwardness, my peers seemed to appreciate my musical abilities and the perceived courage it took to stand up and share something so intimate in front of the entire school. If church was my first experience of the connection possible through song, singing in high school was the second big, formative milestone of such an experience. I still believe that musical experiences can be so powerful that they can help awkward, closeted queer teens find connection with their most unlikely peers.

By my junior year of high school, many of the upperclassmen I'd looked up to and become close with had graduated and left the school, and it was around this time that Jeannie and I found the close-knit group of kids who would become our best friends in the latter half of high school. Once again, I can only credit Jeannie with introducing me to these folks. Whereas I limited myself to those who had made it into my group of familiar faces, Jeannie relished opportunities to befriend anyone new, even if all they had in common was a shared class.

One of the after-school clubs we both attended regularly was poetry club. Poetry club was exactly what it sounds like: a group of teenagers meeting after school in a quiet corner of the library with a teacher to share clumsy and angst-ridden poems with one another. This club attracted teens in two flavors of awkward: shy or theatrical. Generally speaking, neither hailed from the "in crowd".

It was in poetry club that I met Katie and Paul, who were dating at the time, and through the lovebirds, was introduced to Rob and Daniel, inseparable siblings. Sophie, the aforementioned goth extraordinaire, also spent time with this crew. These kids were all creatives of some sort, although most of them weren't members of the choir or band. We were all interested in music, anything deemed "alternative," and fancied ourselves "deep thinkers." Soon enough, we all began hanging out at Katie's house, where I'd play songs on her parents' upright piano. I was a great sight-reader, and she had tons of songbooks I didn't have at home, so I learned to play a sizable chunk of Billy Joel's and Elton John's catalog on these late nights.

We'd all attend grungy punk shows at the local VFW (Veterans of Foreign Wars) club on weekend nights, where we'd mosh and thrash to loud, sloppy high school bands from neighboring towns. We'd don our finest fishnet, combat boots, torn jeans, and eyeliner and just hurl our bodies around to the pure ecstasy, anger, pain, and joy of it all. Eventually Paul, Rob, Daniel, and I decided to form a band, but the only places we ever really played were Katie's garage and my parents' living room (much to their chagrin), and we only ever really played cover songs from the guys' favorite band at the time, AFI. For my seventeenth birthday, I dressed these sweet, usually unremarkably-dressed straight boys in all the pleather, fishnet, spikes, and skin-tight polyester I had. I did their makeup before we all shook the living room walls of the parsonage where I lived with our loud, poorly-tuned, hardcore punk/emo sounds.

In those last two years of high school, and their corresponding summers, these folks became my family. I can't remember much of anything from these years, save for the hours spent at either Katie's or Daniel and Rob's houses in the neighboring town of Mount Laurel. We sang songs, platonically cuddled (although I did have the hardest of crushes on Daniel, who was two years my junior and dating Jeannie at the time), climbed trees, joked endlessly, and shared deeply.

While none of these folks, save myself and Jeannie, identified as anything but straight, this was my queer family. These were the people who saw me and whom I saw in turn, and we shared just about everything a group of people could share. We felt everything so deeply and completely, and then one day, a year into college, I was in my first "serious" relationship, and we just stopped seeing one another. My boyfriend (and eventual first husband) felt as though we should do everything together, and thought that "being serious" meant relying solely on one another and making friends together, and since he didn't quite connect with my friends, I suppose that meant that they had to go.

A couple of years ago, I reconnected with Katie over social media while I drummed up some interest for a show I'd be playing in Philly. She brought her parents along to my show and we reminisced about the late nights at her place. I found myself thinking back on the evenings I had spent with her and others from the boisterous sing-alongs to the quieter moments like when Daniel strummed his acoustic guitar. On my subsequent tour stop in Philly the following year, I took the chance of sending him a message on Facebook. He was living outside of Philadelphia with a wife and two children. Seeing him at the small queer house show where I played in West Philadelphia healed my inner teen goth.

This summer, I was booked to open for a local Philly songwriter at Johnny Brenda's, an old indie rock venue in the Fishtown neighborhood. Daniel and Katie both showed up, making a point to join me before the show for some pizza at a nearby joint. Something felt full circle about finally playing a "real" venue in my old hometown, and having two of my oldest friends in the audience, smiling up at me as I sang the song they and our adventures together as teenagers inspired.

Study questions

1. Thinking alongside CJ Pascoe's *Dude you're a fag: masculinity and sexuality in high school* (2007), examine how DeSilva's relationships with her peers complicates the *fag discourse* that Pascoe uses to describe the hierarchies of after-school activities like drama clubs.

6
The devil in New Jersey

The devil in New Jersey

Fly over the pines of south Jersey
Past the traffic on I-95
It hurts so much now, but you're learning
Life's more than staying alive.

They say the devil's in New Jersey
And god damn if they weren't right.
All of the searching made you worry
Hiding in shadows, and ducking out of sight.

Fly over the pines of south Jersey
Past the traffic on I-95
It hurts so much now, but you're learning
Life's more than staying alive.

He wasn't invited to your potluck
His piety dressed in Sunday's worst.
He poisoned your macaroni salad

Just dealing gossip, in a scripture verse.

Fly over the pines of south Jersey
Past the traffic on I-95
It hurts so much now, but you're learning
Life's more than staying alive.

You turned a gentle boy into a demon
Relegated to his room
Hid behind a broken down piano
Singing for acceptance
And praying to the moon.

Fly over the pines of south Jersey
Past the traffic on I-95
It hurts so much now, but you're learning
Life's more than staying alive.

They say the devil's in New Jersey
And god damn if they weren't right.

I came out to my parents in the early months of 1998. More accurately, I was forced out by their suspicions. My part in the saga began with an evening dinner with my father. I'm not sure why I felt so caught off guard – while my dad and I had a friendly relationship, this was probably the first time he'd ever taken me out for dinner, just the two of us, but despite my increasing secrecy at this point in my adolescence, I still craved the warmth and closeness with my parents we'd enjoyed in years gone by.

My dad took me to my favorite Italian restaurant in the next town over Medford, New Jersey. Previously this was a spot reserved for special occasions like birthdays or anniversaries, but as far as I knew, this night was just a "father and son" bonding dinner. We talked like buddies over our meal, expressing our joys and concerns for my mom and sisters, and discussing music we'd both been enjoying recently. I was allowed to order the lobster ravioli in vodka sauce, so I knew my dad must have been in a great mood. He asked about school. I told him my grades were just fine, and that I was making new friends with some of the upperclassmen I'd met in concert choir.

It wasn't until we were sitting in the car in the parking lot preparing to leave that he dropped the bomb. I remember feeling the energy change when he didn't immediately shift into drive to take us home. "The talk" was coming and as much as I'd have loved to give over to the waters of fear and shame in my mind and just let myself drown, I felt myself paddling frantically to stay afloat.

It was a notebook of poems and drawings that did it in the end. Something I'd kept safe, just for myself. A private space for my thoughts, feelings, and reflections. I'd begun going to poetry club once a week after school with Jeannie and had discovered the life-saving catharsis of poetry and songwriting. The funniest part about this was that other than the scandalous drawings I'd been doodling, my own inner historian had been my ultimate liability.

I'd always had a rich inner life and fantasy world as a child, and this was not something I truly grew out of in adolescence. I spent many an afternoon watching shows like "Behind the Music" and "Storytellers" on VH1, and at this point I was convinced I'd be a rock star someday, somehow. When I began collecting poems and lyrics in my little spiral-bound notebook, I had the idea that perhaps someday it would become an important archive of my early years, and so I included footnotes under each poem with the date of composition and a sentence or two about who or what it was about. There were many embarrassingly adolescent verses about a couple of the older boys I'd developed feelings for in my first year of high school. These annotations would provide unquestionable evidence of my developing sexuality were anyone to find them.

I spent years blaming my mother for searching through my bedroom and flipping through this notebook. Truth be told, there is probably a part of me that still holds a bit of resentment.

After all, it felt like a violation of the most vulnerable parts of myself. Of course, in spite of the story she told, I would **never** leave this precious notebook open on my bed with the door open for anyone to just waltz in and find it. I had a secret hiding place deep in my closet, of all places. I still wonder, though, if part of me thought it might be easier if she just "found out" this way. Maybe that's the real reason I added all of these revealing notes in the margins of the pages. I don't think at that point I'd planned to ever come out to my parents. I had assumed that at some point, my relationship with them would have to come to an end if I were ever to want to live openly. Perhaps that was why I still held on to whatever relationship I was able to have with them at the time.

Regardless, there I was, cornered in the passenger seat of my dad's old Chevy Beretta, his eyes almost pleading for me to explain that this was all just a big misunderstanding. And so I did it. I came out. Well, almost.

"So… are you gay? What does this all mean?" My father's voice shook as his eyes went wide with concern.

"No! Yes. I don't know… I know I am attracted to guys…" I searched his face and could only see fear staring back. "… but… I think I may still like girls too. I-I'm really struggling."

I was not struggling. I was completely out as gay with my friends at school, and I'd already had my first kiss with the only other gay kid I knew at school at the time, in one of the small music practice rooms between the choir room and the band room. I knew who I was with regard to my sexuality by the time my father and I had this uncomfortable conversation. I was just so afraid of disappointing him that I felt like I needed to give him one more thread of hope to cling to. I knew where his religious beliefs stood, and I thought that if I said I was struggling with these feelings, perhaps I could ease my way out of the closet.

Over the next year or so, my father and I maintained a system of communication that worked for us. Talking face to face was always difficult for both of us, especially when the topics of conversation were difficult, and we both considered ourselves more adept with the written word in terms of conveying our thoughts and emotions. We would leave letters for each other every week or so – I'd leave mine on my dad's desk in his home office, and he would leave his atop my chest of drawers in my bedroom (of course I had an "open door" policy now). In these letters, we would keep each other up to date on where we both were with "the issue." Coupled with his usual praying, my dad, ever the researcher, began reading ferociously. He sought out religious texts from LGBTQ-affirming Christian theologians rather than further entrenching himself in the bigoted theology he already knew so well.

My mother and I didn't speak for at least two weeks after my fateful dinner with my father. It felt like my very presence in the same room pained her beyond the point of speech, and she would often cry when we passed each other in the house. Although I had every right to be angry with her invasion of my privacy, I really just wanted the comfort and familiarity of my mother. I wanted to watch trashy daytime TV with her and laugh the way we always had. I felt so alone and was certain that she was disgusted with me. As it turned out, she just needed time to sit with her feelings and adjust to the fact that her child was not going to have the future she'd envisioned. When we did eventually speak, she shared the fear that I would be mistreated and unsafe because of my queerness, and that this, rather than any moral issue, was the hardest thing for her to come to terms with.

Eventually in one of those letters to my father, I shared that I was not really struggling with my own sexuality, but rather with how and when to rip off the Band-Aid. It wasn't easy, but it was easier in writing, without his pleading eyes in front of mine, to finally say what I'd known for a long time – I was gay. I liked boys and I always had, and I had been out to my friends at school for months and felt loved and supported by them. With my permission, he shared this with my mom and eventually, a year or so later, with my younger sisters as well. At the time, I gladly accepted his offer to be my interlocutor, but years later I'd wonder why he hadn't wanted me to speak with them myself. I think now that he was perhaps protecting me. He's always been a bit of a mediator, and I think he felt as though he could handle whatever ways the rest of my family would respond and smooth things over if need be, before anything was able to reach me. If nothing else, the coming out experience had brought my dad and me closer together, and it was a closeness we would need to endure the turmoil ahead.

In the summer of 2000 we were all enjoying our yearly family vacation to Cape May, New Jersey. Growing up on my dad's meager preacher's salary, we didn't have much, but he always did his best to save for (or go into debt for) our summer week "down the shore." Cape May was the destination of choice because it held special childhood memories for my mom. We'd walk down picturesque, tree-lined streets and fantasize about what it would be like to stay in one of the many old Victorian mansions there. Mom would always stop and tell us about the house her grandparents had stayed in when she was a kid, and she'd usually get a bit teary before we teased her gently about it. We'd browse the artsy shops, enjoy ice cream and arcade games on the boardwalk, and return to the small condo we'd rented to enjoy the evenings together on the porch, my mom with a cocktail my dad had made for her, and he with a cigar in hand.

These vacations were small pockets of refuge for all of us. My dad always struggled with his sense of identity in the church, and at the time, he still served a fairly conservative congregation, many of whom didn't even know that he smoked cigars or enjoyed the occasional glass of wine. My mother struggled similarly with the role of pastor's wife that she'd never really asked for, and I found the role of dutiful preacher's "son" increasingly difficult. My sisters were still young enough that I'd like to think they were immune to such things, but if they were, their immunity was on borrowed time.

On one of those lazy June evenings (we would usually go on vacation as early in the season as we could, to get the best rental rates), while we were blissfully drinking in the warmth of the air and each other's company, my dad received a phone call that immediately drained all the sun-kissed color from his face. It wasn't unusual for him to receive calls on vacation, usually with news that an older congregant was sick or had just died. He'd had to leave many times to drive home for a funeral, and this time his alabaster face left us concerned about the unusual gravity of whomever had died. No one had died.

That spring some of my queer and ally friends and I had founded the first Gay-Straight Alliance (GSA) at our large, regional high school. We'd all been so proud of being able to establish a safe space like this, with real, actual adult teachers who willingly served as supportive mentors. Lenape High School in Medford, New Jersey served multiple townships in Burlington County and had such a large student body that you could go all four years without having seen – much less met or become acquainted with – every other student in attendance. This was one of the blessings of my high school career; the size of the school shielded me from the torturous harassment many queer kids of my generation had to endure. When the school newspaper decided to write an article about the GSA, my friends and I were thrilled.

Maybe that way we could reach students who weren't aware of its existence and help others feel safe enough to come out.

Much like I'd spent years avoiding thinking about whether I'd ever come out to my parents, perhaps my parents had also chosen to dismiss the issue of the church's response to my queerness with an "out-of-sight, out-of-mind" approach. They knew about the GSA and the article in the school paper, and had been nothing but proud and supportive of me. What all of us had neglected to consider was that there were younger kids in the church youth group who'd begun attending my school that year. Furthermore, the school paper went home with every student, just like report cards and permission slips, and one of the parents of these church kids had seen the article and immediately started a phone chain to inform the entire church of the news that the preacher's kid was, at best, friends with gay kids, and at worst, one of the deviants himself.

For years leading up to this fateful summer of 2000, my father maintained that he could do greater good by remaining in the American Baptist Association rather than jumping ship and swimming to more progressive religious shores. Rather than push his evolving, more progressive theology on his congregation, he believed that he could ease them in the right direction. He'd favored sermons that challenged his congregants to be more charitable in showing God's love, and while he'd not tackled "the issue of homosexuality" overtly in his sermons, he'd moved actively against the practice of condemning anyone from the pulpit. With this phone call, it seemed that there were some who would force his hand.

When we returned from our vacation, an emergency meeting was called with my father and the board of church deacons. The meeting lasted longer than planned as my mother, sisters, and I nervously flipped through television channels to distract ourselves. The parsonage where we lived was less than 20 feet from the church itself, and the dread and tension left no inch spared. I will never forget the fear, hurt, and anger evident on my dad's face when he walked through the back door into our TV room that night.

There was one man named Carl who was the most vicious and vocal in the room where my father had basically stood on trial for the sin of loving his gay child. Red-faced and blustering, Carl had accused my father of being "in league with the Devil," while also referring to me as the Devil incarnate. A few others joined Carl in wondering aloud whether it might not be safe for me to be around the children in the congregation, lest I become predatory toward younger children or influence my peers to join the dark side themselves. Some of the men in the room accused my father of hiding his own views on homosexuality as sin, and when he tried to explain that his views had changed, Carl shot back: "God doesn't change. Sin is sin."

What I think hurt my dad most wasn't Carl's desperate anger, but rather the stony-faced silence of those he'd thought of as friends, if not trusted allies. There were a select few in the church with whom he'd felt that he could breathe a little more deeply and share at least a hint of himself beyond his role as pastor. Every single one of these people remained silent. In the end, he left with an ultimatum: condemn homosexuality in a sermon, in front of the entire congregation, or leave.

The ultimatum in question was, thankfully, never really a question for my father. He told me that very night that, even if his views on homosexuality had not evolved to a place of acceptance, he would not use his position as a preacher to publicly condemn his child. I was entering my senior year in high school, and so we would stay to allow me and my sisters to finish out the next academic year, while my father would begin the process of searching for a new congregation. He was beaten down and tired of the life he'd chosen, but he felt at this point that these were the only skills he could use to support his family. I think there was part of him that felt more galvanized to try to be a voice for change in the American Baptist Association.

My mom and I attended church events with purposeful infrequency that year. Whenever I would attend, for a holiday or to support my dad, I'd adorn myself in all of my queer goth finery: dark smudged eyeliner, black painted nails, pleather pants, and bright pink hair. If they wanted to make me a devil, I'd lean into it. I'd embrace the things that made them scared of me. It was a stark contrast to the life I'd lived in the church up until this point. Church was where I'd learned to sing. It was where I'd felt the alluring embrace of the slightest hint of celebrity – "The pastor's son is so talented! What an amazing young man of God!" This seductive, surface-level acceptance, no matter how at odds with my true self, was something I grieved, and I eventually distanced myself from the church altogether, counting the days until I could graduate and go to college in Philadelphia – the nearest "big city."

These months became a defining era for my family. While it gal-
vanized my father to make whatever small waves of accepting
change he could in his corner of Christianity, it cemented the
bitterness my mother had toward the hypocrisy of church life,
and the role she was thrust into as a preacher's wife. My younger
sister Sarah had to leave her two closest friends just as she began
her adolescence, and my youngest sister Abbey found a passion
for social justice and allyship even at her young age. While I was
comforted by the stand my family took, I felt as though they
undertook all of this tribulation **because of me**. I'd spent most
of my childhood trying to make myself invisible through good
behavior and a persona of being "mature for my age." I'd allowed
myself one small space of indulgence in the limelight afforded to
me as a singer, but even that I'd done under the guise of a chaste,
Christian life that was not mine.

Years later in adulthood, I remembered an episode of *The X
Files* I'd caught on television as a teenager, in which the "case"
Agents Mulder and Scully took on was that of the infamous
Jersey Devil. I remembered the thrill of seeing a vague – if not
inaccurate – version of my home state portrayed on screen. The
Pine Barrens where all of the aforementioned events had taken
place in a sandy, rural region in southern New Jersey, beginning
in Burlington County where we lived and extending southeast
to the coast. This region is apparently the home of the folkloric
Jersey Devil, a cryptid whose tales extend to the late eighteenth
century.

I've always been fascinated by the dark, the mystical, and the
occult, and was reminded of the tale of the Jersey Devil a few
years back, while listening to one of the many creepy podcasts

I enjoy on long drives and the occasional run. As with all such tales, origins and reported sightings of the devil are fiercely debated. Some say that the devil was the conjuration of a witch, while others portray it as the result of an unwanted pregnancy. In almost every telling however, the Jersey Devil flees the scene, and remains clandestine. Like Bigfoot, the Jersey Devil, it seems, just wants to be left alone.

I think, as a queer teenager in the late 1990s, who was confronted regularly with their identity as a "hot button debate," I just craved a sense of normalcy. I didn't **want** to hide, so much as I wanted my identity to be a non-issue. I didn't spend much time prior to 1998 thinking about how I'd come out, because I fiercely resented that I **had** to. By the time my father's congregants arrived with their tongues shaped as pitchforks and torches, my family, friends, and I had begun to build what felt like a mundane sense of normalcy. Life finally felt as close to comfortable for me as it had ever been, despite the "normal" tumult of adolescence. Did I receive dirty looks from kids in school or from the "normies" at the mall where my friends and I hung out on Friday nights? I sure did. I had my community around me, though, and we embraced the dirty looks. My straight friends all donned their best mall-goth finery and we were loud and obnoxious, and there was a power in the scorn we invited from others. What happened in the church at Vincentown felt like a violation. It was something neither I nor my family asked for. It was my first true experience of persecution and marginalization, and it didn't just happen to me alone. It happened to my family. It happened in the one place that was supposed to feel like home. The "family of God."

Suddenly I had been made "the devil." I was no longer the golden child rather, I was a monster. I was just searching for sanctuary wherever I could find it, and if I could not, I was forced to fly away over the pines of Burlington County, New Jersey. When I wrote "The Devil in New Jersey," I joked at first that I never thought I'd write a song about Carl, a man who had caused my family such pain, but in the end, the song isn't for him. Of course it's about how religious-sanctioned hatred turns the pious into the real monster, but more so, it's a song for the monster who is hunted. It's a song for the person I'd for so long refused to see in that saga of my family's history: me.

7
Glitter up the dark

Glitter up the dark

They caught you out there in your fishnets honey
Way before it was cool
Under the shadow of the Whitman Bridge
One of those evenings after school.

Probably had a little sass to serve 'em
Probably met them with a smile
I bet you read 'em all to filth now baby
Bet it still keeps them up at night.

How do you glitter up the dark?
Glitter when they block out the light?
Maybe your battle with your shadows
Makes you sparkle brighter at night.
Teach me to glitter up the dark…
Glitter up the dark…
Glitter up the dark.

All that trauma and depression baby
Was handed down just like your eyes
All of the beauty of your joy and rage
You held it all at the same time.

That's how I see you still today now honey
Although the vision's less than clear.
A gritty saint decked out in full beat baby
Your sense of humor as your shield.

How do you glitter up the dark?
Glitter when they block out the light?
Maybe your battle with your shadows
Makes you sparkle brighter at night
Teach me to glitter up the dark…

You'd always take a little spark
Light it in the dark
You'd turn the ugly into pretty
Something witty just to take off the edge
Bring you down off the ledge.

How do you glitter up the dark?
Glitter when they block out the light?
Maybe your battle with your shadows
Makes you sparkle brighter at night
Teach me to glitter up the dark…
Glitter up the dark…
Glitter up the dark.

I met Spark when I was 16. I'd recently come out to my parents, and one of the few openly queer kids at my school was hosting a gathering at his house to be led by an adult representative of a queer youth center called The Attic in Philadelphia, which was the closest major city to my home in southern New Jersey.

The only queer kids I had ever met up until this point were my best friend Jeannie, Chris, who was hosting the gathering and whom I'd "dated" for two days earlier in the school year, and an upperclassman named Dennis who sang bass in the school choir. Since Jeannie and Chris were both at this gathering, along with two or three other kids from neighboring school districts, this was officially the largest gathering of queer folks I'd ever attended.

I don't remember much from this gathering. At the time I was still convinced that Chris was "the one who got away," and spent most of the evening trying to make eye contact with him, even though it's clear to me now that we were completely incompatible and he was simply one of two other gay guys in my high school. I still hadn't found my "style" at this point. I'd no doubt put on my coolest puka shell choker and gelled my hair to the point of no return. Despite my sartorial armor, I was still pretty shy in groups of kids I didn't know, so I likely spent most of the evening brooding and trying to be invisible to everyone but Chris.

Jeannie was a flame that attracted weirdos and outcasts to her like moths. Not even a week had passed before she'd already spent countless late-night hours on the phone with the kids we'd met that evening. Spark was the one with whom she'd connected best. Spark was the skinny goth kid who'd sat across from me in the circle of chairs that evening, and despite his unique appearance, I recall that he was fairly quiet as well. He'd joined the group from a city called Gloucester, which neighbored Camden and sat in the shadow of the Walt Whitman Bridge, just across the river from Philadelphia.

One night, during one of our many late night phone calls, Jeannie mischievously said, "Someone has a crush on you."

Now, I've always been someone who is utterly oblivious to any affections directed my way, and even when a third party reveals something like this, I tend to deflect or outright refuse to believe them. When Jeannie got that tone in her voice, my stomach fluttered with the hope that either Chris's feelings were rekindled, or perhaps even Dennis from choir had finally seen the light… but it wasn't either of them.

"Remember Spark?" Jeannie said.

"Who?" Now I almost worried that she'd been playing some sort of trick on me. Jeannie would never be so cruel, though.

"Spark, from the group at Chris's house the other night. We've been talking. He's **so** funny and **so** cute, and he told me he really likes you. I'm gonna hang out with him at the Moorestown Mall this Friday if you want to come. Oh, and he wanted me to give you his number."

If I'm completely honest, I had paid next to no attention to Spark at Chris's house, but immediately my heart began to race. My adolescent yearning for requited love and my having been starved for queer community in late-1990s New Jersey were such that I immediately felt like he was **the one**. What a sweet story this would be to tell my future grandchildren! Sure, Spark lived 40 minutes away by car and I couldn't drive, but I'd seen plenty of romcoms in my young life, and I knew we could make this work.

With Jeannie's coaching, I eventually hung up our call and dialed Spark's number on my family's cordless phone. Jeannie and

I lived in the same town and had the same area code: 609, so phone calls were free, but I'd have to come up with some excuse for my parents as to why I'd called someone with an 856 number. Better to beg forgiveness than ask for permission. I was out to my parents but it was still an uneasy truce, and I wasn't ready to talk about boys with them yet.

Soon enough, Spark and I were spending hours on the phone with one another. I was enchanted by his free spirit, his sense of humor, and the way he seemed so much more experienced and worldly than me (even though he was seven months younger). He was quick- witted and would talk a mile a minute, hurling references to bands I'd never listened to, and even drag queens I'd never heard of. This was more than a decade before *RuPaul's Drag Race*, and in the internet's infancy, so how he'd come across Varla Jean Merman I'll never know. Spark was the gayest, most interesting person I had ever met at that point in my young life. How could someone so vivacious and cool be interested in me?

Over the next four months, Spark and I "dated," which, in late 1990s, teenage terms meant, we wrote letters (yes, literal letters we sent through the mail), spoke on the phone (no, not a cell phone. Neither of us had those yet), and saw each other on Friday nights at the Moorestown Mall, which was about halfway between both of our homes. My parents would drive me, and Spark would take the bus.

Jeannie was usually present for those glorious Friday night mall hangs, as well as a bunch of kids from other neighboring towns, all of whom knew Spark. All of these kids fell into the categories of "mall goth," "skater boy," or "raver princess," and Spark and Jeannie held court as *de facto* queens. These kids seemed so much freer in the ways they talked, moved, and especially in the ways they dressed. I immediately felt that strange pressure to conform to this newfound nonconformity. Soon enough I was being styled by Spark, with newly bleached hair and kitschy accessories from a mall shop called Claire's that marketed itself to teenage girls.

Spark was everything I wanted to be and I couldn't really distinguish between the desire to be with him and the desire to be just like him.

These few hours every Friday night were my first taste of freedom from the watchful eyes of my parents, the church, or schoolteachers, and I was determined to soak in as much of it as possible. Spark and I stole kisses in the bushes outside the mall, and rushed through anxious handjobs in the dark of the movie theater. We and our comrades were loud and intrusive, and we made the "mall cops'" lives a living hell at every opportunity. They would follow us into stores where we would loudly taunt them for thinking we were going to steal – of course they were judging us because we were different! They just didn't understand us because we were freaks and goths!

One night I proudly got kicked out of the mall for loudly and dramatically pretending to trip repeatedly, which my adolescent insolence found **hilarious**. We were menaces and I have no doubt that I would roll my middle-aged eyes at such displays were I to see us frolicking about today.

Through all of this, all I could taste was the sweetness of refusing to follow the rules.

I'd been a rule-follower all my life. I was so afraid of disappointing my parents, my teachers, God even, and the knowledge that I was different only seemed to magnify my own isolation. I'd spent all of my 16 years trying to feel special without sacrificing my parents' love, and only very recently had I challenged that notion of "goodness." Here was a group of kids my age who reveled in being different and being "bad," all while pointing out the silliness and hypocrisy of those who judged them. They owned their queerness, their depression, the fact that they'd been medicated for most of their lives by their parents; many of them had even endured unthinkable abuse. In comparison, my childhood felt embarrassingly quaint.

Eventually I came clean to my parents that Spark and I were "boyfriends." They were trying so hard to be supportive, as they dropped me off at his home in Gloucester on Halloween. Spark came prancing off his front porch in fishnet stockings, combat boots, a black mesh top, full glitter goth makeup, a black tulle skirt, and a pair of fairy wings, and I could feel my father hold his breath as I opened the car door. Not many fathers would allow their gay teenage kid to spend the weekend with their boyfriend, much less a Baptist pastor.

It was during this weekend stay that I really began to see Spark, beyond the sparkly, cheery, dry-humored persona he donned publicly. This isn't to say that any of it was a façade by any means, but it also seemed to be a coping mechanism for the many difficulties he'd been dealt in his young life.

Being a Baptist pastor was not (for my father at least) a lucrative pursuit. My family had subsisted at times with the aid of food stamps, but my parents also had access to things like credit. We were able to experience a veneer of comfortable middle class, no doubt because of the respectability politics that come with being a religious clergy member.

It was clear even upon driving into the city limits of Gloucester that this poverty was different from the more rural suburban brand I'd grown up with. Spark's circumstances were more financially precarious. He had never known his father, and lived with his mother and aunt, both of whom suffered from physical and mental health ailments. Spark had disclosed multiple mental health diagnoses to me, as well as a history of anorexia and self-harm, and at least one recent stay in a mental health institution. I'd been dealing with my own increased restriction of food due to body dysmorphia as well as incidents of self-harm, but Spark always portrayed himself as having "survived" these things and come out all the wiser and stronger for it. He was always protective of me and cried at the thought that I would mistreat myself in these ways. One time, he hinted at an incident of having been beaten by some neighborhood boys down by the train tracks, but he always followed such revelations with a sharply-timed joke that made him seem invincible to me.

I too felt invincible by Spark's side. We went trick-or-treating during the daylight hours that weekend, Spark dressed in his goth fairy costume and me in full baby drag as grunge-era Courtney Love. I'd borrowed a baby doll dress from my friend Cindy, platform Mary Jane shoes and fishnet stockings from Jeannie, and had bought a cheap blonde wig and a beauty queen tiara from Spencer's in the mall. We marched defiantly up and down the streets of Gloucester, NJ, past the bullies who had beaten Spark for being gay, as well as countless other befuddled teenagers and adults. In retrospect, we were definitely not safe, but I never felt anything but protected while holding his hand. It was as if the power of his shining presence was a force field against the bigotry surrounding us. But sauntering through the streets of Gloucester was only a thrilling vacation for me. My parents would pick me up the next day, and I would wake in the relative safety of my house and return to my well-resourced, top-rated regional high school on Monday, to disappear among the throngs of the large student body, where I would enjoy choir class and art studio. Spark lived in Gloucester. He would have to meet those same bullies on the street, perhaps while walking alone. The obliviousness of my sheltered privilege is astoundingly obvious to me now.

During the brief time we were together, Spark was my bridge into queer and alternative cultures. I watched my first queer films with him, including the British film *Beautiful Thing* (1996) and for the first time, I allowed myself to dream of a world in which I might live openly and in love. He made me countless mix tapes, introducing me to bands like Rasputina, Garbage, and The Wannadies, and I listened through the rough, dark sounds to hear my teenage heartache and yearning reflected back at me. Spark was also the first person I had sex with, and despite all of the fumbling, teenage awkwardness with which we tend to look back on these experiences, he was nothing but gentle, protective, and focused on enthusiastic consent (perhaps informed by his own traumatic experiences). My brief teenage romance with Spark was formative for me in ways I'm still discovering.

Eventually, our differences became less and less charming. My timid teenage rebellion had its limits, it seems, as there was also a rift growing between Jeannie and me. My ignorance wasn't cute when it wandered into the realm of judgment, and as so many teenagers do, Spark and I found we had less in common than we had once thought. From what I remember, Spark broke up with me, although I can't recall exactly why, but I do remember the enormity of the heartache. I basked in the glorious pain of Tori Amos' dark and shocking "Boys for Pele" album, which I played on repeat in my bedroom as I reread all of the sweet teenage love letters Spark had written me in the previous months. I listened over and over again to mix tapes he'd made for me, trying to decipher some subtext in the song lyrics to offer a glimmer of hope that we might reconcile. And then of course, life continued.

* * *

Time is a slippery thing, especially upon recollection. A year passes in the blink of an eye, and a four-month-long teenage relationship feels like a decade-long love affair. Spark and I stayed in touch and even hung out "as friends" a few times before I graduated high school. These were dark years for him, and we'd drift in and out of each other's lives many times. While I continued to go to school, take the SATs, and apply for college, Spark endured sex work, addictions, and more than what he ever let on.

We eventually reunited a couple of years later when I was in an increasingly serious relationship with Brad, the man who would become my first husband. Spark had paid his way through cosmetology school and began regularly cutting our hair and hanging out to talk afterward. We'd moved to Philadelphia, where Brad and I were both working at a bank while I pursued a bachelor's degree in music at Temple University. Spark had been living in a tiny apartment across town and we began seeing more and more of each other. As had always been the case, I trusted him with my life and, by extension, my hair, and would usually let him do whatever he liked with it. His skills had come a long way since the time he'd bleached my hair in high school before we went to my homecoming dance together.

Spark's sense of humor had always been chaotic and his tendency toward mile-a-minute, disjunct chatter hadn't changed. I knew he had been through a lot and I'd chalked up most of his erratic behavior to mental health struggles, and Spark just "being Spark," but the more he needed to borrow money or crash on our couch after being evicted or breaking up with another guy, the clearer it became that there might be more going on. I'd never really known the extent of Spark's drug use, much less the specifics of what he'd been using, but it turned out that he'd been using heroin and things were worse than I'd imagined. Regardless of what had been going on in his own life, he prioritized asking me how I had been, and always found the energy to make me laugh hysterically.

After a long stretch with no signs of Spark, he finally called to tell me that he had been in rehab for his heroin use, and was a couple of months clean. I could feel the brightness of his shine through the phone line, as he shifted the focus to how I had been, asked after Brad, and threw in his typical sharp-witted zingers to make me laugh. Underneath it all was a new layer of world-weariness that gave me pause, but I was relieved to have my friend back.

Spark had lost many of his friends in pursuit of his sobriety, and although he still checked in and cared for his mother, it seemed more that she relied on him than the other way around.

One evening, after our usual haircut and catch-up, Spark got quiet. After a beat, he asked Brad and me if we would accompany him to his local N.A. (Narcotics Anonymous) meeting. In a rare moment of earnestness, he explained that the meetings were what kept him alive and sober – particularly since testing positive for HIV – and he had just reached his first full year of sobriety. He said that we were his family, and he wanted to share the milestone with us. I got the sense that he'd wanted to ask us before, but perhaps felt embarrassed.

Later that night, after the N.A. meeting (in a church basement somewhere in South Philly), the three of us sat comfortably in a booth at a Thai restaurant on South Street. We laughed, of course, as we always did – one couldn't help but roar with laughter around Spark – but we also talked openly and sincerely maybe for the first time since Spark and I had dated in high school. It was like a seal had been broken during the N.A. meeting, allowing us to drop the pretenses and the need for humor to lighten the mood. Spark had spoken candidly in the meeting about things he'd been through that I'd only inferred but that he'd never told me until that point. I was so proud of him and I told him that.

* * *

A few years later I'd once again lost touch with Spark. Our phone calls became increasingly sporadic, and when we did speak, I mostly listened as he rattled on at breakneck speed delivering often incoherent narratives of all that he had been going through.

Despite his protestations, I feared that he was using again, and while this would not have been his first relapse, it would be the last that I would be present for. He'd reached a place where he only seemed to reach out when he needed money, a place to stay, or even just a warm body to sit on the other end of the phone line while he talked at them. His sparkle seemed to have dimmed to an occasional spark – the struggling rev of a dying car battery being futilely charged. I'd reached a place where I felt like my friend was no longer a friend, and soon I stopped taking or returning his calls. I am still trying to forgive myself for this.

In early October 2016, just after his 32nd birthday, I received a phone call from Spark's closest childhood friend. My stomach dropped as I wondered why she might be calling after so much time, and as I answered, she tearfully told me that Spark had died. The last person who seemed to have spoken with him had been Brad. He and I had separated some time before, and it seems as though he was the one person who had remained in touch with Spark, although, by the very end Brad had also lost the ability to contact him. At this point, he was homeless, in and out of shelters, and likely using again. I am not sure that I will ever be able to move past the knowledge that Spark was completely alone when he died.

* * *

In the spring of 2017, I had been teaching at The University of the Arts in Philadelphia, and one of the courses I'd been assigned was to co-teach the senior Musical Theatre cabaret class. As I urged students each class to bring themselves to the stories they told through song, I found myself reflecting on my own life. I decided to write and perform a solo cabaret, with songs by Stevie Nicks and stories that drew from the pivotal moments in my life.

As I sat down to collect my stories and songs, I found myself coming back time and again to the joy and pain of growing up queer. I wanted to express the beauty of queerness, and whenever that is the aim, I find myself thinking of Spark. I'd decided that I wanted to pay tribute to him somehow through this performance, as he was the brightest, shiniest, most complex person I'd known and loved, and so I decided that the show would be a benefit for The Attic Youth Center, the organization that had been a lifeline for him in his youth, and that introduced me to one of the greatest friends I've ever had.

The performance itself was one of the most liberating and joyful I've ever experienced. Through college and grad school, I'd fallen mostly into performing Western classical music, and singing in operas – which had mostly felt like telling other people's stories. By 2017 I'd been losing my love for this sort of performing, and the Stevie Nicks cabaret was the first time in years, maybe ever, that I'd felt so fully myself onstage. In many ways, collecting my stories and telling them through song would lead to my renewed interest in songwriting, which would, in a roundabout way, lead to the book you are reading right now. And still, all these years later, I find myself learning from Spark to embrace the fullness of my traumatized and complex, queer self.

Study questions

1. How does DeSilva's relationship with Spark resonate with the concept of "queer futurity" as theorized by José Esteban Muñoz in his 2009 book *Cruising Utopia: The Then and There of Queer Futurity*?

8
Family tree

Family tree

Your laugh is a song I haven't heard in years
But I can still sing every word.
It floats into my head sometimes and I smile
'Cuz I know you're in the world.

Seasons change like friends and lovers
And other people you hold dear.
Some folks are there to build you, others hold you,
Keep you standing through the years.

Neighbor, lover, father, friend
Isn't it about love in the end?

Chorus:
We're building a family tree
With borrowed branches
The best and the worst of me.
Oh what a recipe
Woven into the fabric
Of our canopy.
Building a family tree.

So open all the windows and the doors
And let the springtime in.
Look at all you've grown from what you've sewn
Before the winter's child.

Sister, mother, teacher, friend.
Isn't it about love in the end?

(Chorus)

For all my talk of chosen kin
And loving from the outside in
Even if I had the chance to choose
I want you to know that I'd still pick you.

(Chorus)

When my spouse and I decided to get married, it wasn't initially out of some need to make our love official in front of "God and our community." I'd already had one go at marriage and divorce myself, and Andrés was wary of the heteronormative, capitalist implications of legal marriage. We were partners in life, and we didn't feel particularly pulled to institutionalize our relationship, but the simple truth was that Andrés was not a citizen, and his time in graduate school was coming to a close. When we spoke to an immigration lawyer, it seemed as though marriage was a necessary step in allowing him to stay in the country and for us to be together, and so we decided we might as well use this as a reason to get the most important people in our lives together for a party.

Andrés and I went through the process of obtaining a marriage license at City Hall in Philadelphia, which we obtained on a Thursday morning in September 2016, and on the following Saturday we were married in my parents' backyard over a potluck, in front of a small group of family, both chosen and of birth. As we worked with my dad who agreed to officiate a ceremony that would reflect us and our values, we found ourselves becoming increasingly emotionally invested in the process. We decided to eschew any religious rites, as well as to write our vows separately to surprise each other during the actual ceremony, but our favorite aspect of the ceremony was the communal reading we crafted. This began as a way to avoid choosing just a handful of our thirty guests to do a few readings. As we curated the texts that held meaning for us, we realized that our idea of "marriage" was one that was held up and bolstered by community. We didn't want this to be some sort of "us against the world" Romeo and Juliet narrative, but rather one that reflected the belief that we are only as strong as the family and community of which we are a part, and which holds us up in mutual support. The pastiche of readings we pieced together featured excerpts from bell hooks, Kahlil Gibran, Sonia Sotomayor, and Tony Kushner.

Years later, when I wrote "Family Tree," in a group writing session with two married friends of mine, this idea of a family we choose and build was fresh in my mind. My friends had a new infant daughter, who was crawling about as we brainstormed ideas for a song, and I had just agreed to be a sperm donor for two other beautiful queer friends of mine and Andrés.

Although I've never wanted to have children of my own, I found myself overcome by the idea that our friends would want me to contribute in such a meaningful way to the family they were building, and as we talked over dinner, they made it clear that they wanted us to be a presence in their child's life, should fertilization be successful. Andrés and I were not expected to be legally obligated to the child in any way, but our friends hoped that we would be "Untie [a gender-neutral term for uncle/aunt] and Uncle" to them.

As I talked with my songwriting group about all of this, we were struck by the beauty and uniqueness of queer family, and the way the branches of our trees intertwined in complex and less traditional ways. We thought of the complex shared root systems of aspen trees, and likened them to the sort of community we each valued in our lives, and thus our words flowered into lyrics.

When my mother broke her silence weeks after I had come out to my parents, she had not only expressed fear for my safety, but also confessed that she worried my isolation and marginalization would lead to a life defined by loneliness. Indeed, the idea of the "lonely life" queer folks face is a trope we see endlessly played out in popular culture, and in the late 1990s that trope boomed across popular media. But the idea of the "lonely queer life" is premised on the assumption that "there are so few of us," as well as the belief that we have to buck against the world rather than be a part of it in order to live our truth.

I empathized with my mother's fears for me, and I realized that they came from her desire as a mother to see her child grow up safe, happy, and fulfilled. I also realize that many queer folks, myself included, have and do continue to live our truths "in spite of" the world. However, the meaning and love I've found in community with others can and must exist alongside the isolation we often feel. Isn't that an entirely human experience, after all?

* * *

In 2020, in the midst of the COVID-19 pandemic, I was struggling to find meaning in my life as a musician. I had just completed a crowdfunding campaign the previous fall to record my second album at a local studio in Boston and had not even made it halfway through the recording process. It seemed as though the project was dead in the water, and in a larger sense, I wondered if I'd ever play music with other people in a shared space again.

In between online voice lessons with my students from the conservatory where I teach, I began tinkering with my own at-home recording. The lessons themselves drained me, as I attempted to be present for over 20 college students, whose lives were interrupted at such a pivotal developmental moment, all while working through my own intense anxiety and existential crises. I knew nothing about recording technology, but if anything, the pandemic had given me a new appreciation for the hint of connection computers had given me, and I knew I had music I wanted to put out into the world.

I had only returned to writing my own songs and recording in 2018, years after I penned my first awkward teenage songs. College and graduate school had washed away my own sense of creative promise and replaced it with an academic reverence for the music of dead white men, and yet, as I began teaching young musical theatre singers, I felt myself reconnecting with a musical language from my youth and longing for an artistic and creative practice that was entirely my own. Until 2020, that's precisely how I'd pursued my songwriting, recording, and performing – alone. The solitary, "starving" artist, starved not for food, but for creative camaraderie and collaboration.

When I began writing songs again, I found myself really drawn to American roots music – some call it "country," but the greater umbrella of roots, blues, folk, and country is called Americana in the music industry. I was inspired by the success and visibility of Brandi Carlile as a lesbian singer-songwriter who wrote and performed music that often flirted with the "country" flavor, and I was reminded of my teenage love of artists like The Indigo Girls and The Chicks back in the late 1990s. I'd grown up in a Baptist church and always enjoyed music with a bit of a twang to it, but in the rural New Jersey town where I grew up, I also associated "capital C-Country" Music with the bigoted folks who tormented me due to my queerness. Artists like Brandi Carlile reminded me that no one has ownership of a musical style, and that I could claim that music as well as a queer, trans artist.

Just before COVID-19 forced us all indoors, I'd been given a taste of collaboration in the early recording sessions for my EP *Hover*, and this had led to more shows with other musicians – drummers, guitarists, and more – joining me. In the most fittingly cliché manner, life showed me what I'd had just before it was gone, and in the middle of 2020, after a few months of singing songs alone in front of my webcam, I was starved for that beautiful musical synergy only experienced with another human being in real time.

It was during this time of collaborative starvation that I received a Facebook message from a guy named Alex. It seemed as though we had some mutual friends in the local music scene, and he was wondering if I'd like to do a co-songwriting session remotely on Zoom. Up until that point, songwriting was a pretty private and solitary undertaking for me and I found myself nervous about how I should answer this random straight guy who'd messaged me out of nowhere. It wasn't so much that I was protective of my "process," as it was that I was unsure of whether I was actually any good at it. I worried that we'd get together to write, and he'd see that I had no idea what I was doing. Furthermore, songwriting for me meant plumbing the depths of my most sacred private thoughts and, at times, even mining my own trauma. Was this straight dude I'd never met before someone I could feel safe enough to do this with?

Before I replied to Alex's message, I did a deep dive into the music he'd released, as well as a bit of a Google stalk. What I found were some of the most beautifully-written meditations on mental health and trauma, all tied together with aching folk melodies, exquisitely-picked acoustic guitar, and gorgeous string arrangements. Alex's music (released under the moniker Old Tom & The Lookouts) felt like an amalgamation of the classic folk rock I'd grown up with, along with some of the lyrical sensibility and impassioned vocals of my favorite late-nineties emo bands. Armed with all of this new information, I decided to respond, and to accept his invitation to collaborate.

What has come since has been perhaps the most rewarding musical collaboration of my life. Alex and I began to meet weekly – first on Zoom, and eventually in person at his home just west of Boston – to write songs together. We each brought something unique to the table and challenged each other's lyrical and musical sensibilities with the ways we approached our craft. Indeed, many of the songs I've quoted in this book were co-written with Alex, but the most beautiful thing that has come out of this musical collaboration is that I've found a brother in song. How could we not become family after sharing the creative discipline that drives us both to wish for a better world?

When I finally decided to release another EP I'd recorded by myself on my laptop, called *Quarantine Sessions,* I really had no idea how to promote it. I'd only released one album independently before, which received one of the most beautiful write-ups from a queer music journalist on their blog. While I assumed this next release would be no different, I was beginning to wish for greater exposure.

I don't quite remember how it happened, but an up-and-coming nonbinary country artist who went by Adeem the Artist was writing for a queer country music outlet caught wind of *Quarantine Sessions* and gave it a lovely write up in an article on "hidden gems" – releases from artists who flew under the radar. Adeem had only recently been reckoning publicly with their pansexual and nonbinary identities, and invited other nonbinary and trans folks to meet up with them over Zoom to talk about their shared experiences, in the hopes of building community.

Adeem and I had interacted a bit on Twitter by that point, but when we "met" to chat on Zoom, we ended up talking for more than an hour and connecting over so many shared experiences of gender dysphoria. Thus began a sisterhood of sorts, that not only helped to carry me through those trying pandemic months, but also served as a musical mentorship, for which I'm deeply grateful.

Through my friendship with Adeem – and thanks largely to the potential for community that still seemed to be present on Twitter in 2020 and 2021, before it was purchased by everyone's least favorite billionaire and rebranded as "X" – I found myself connecting with other queer, trans, and Black, Indigenous, and people of color musicians, working to find their place in Americana music. Organizations like *The Black Opry* – a collective that seeks to uplift and amplify Black artists in country music – founded by my good friend Holly G, and independent e- zines like *Rainbow Rodeo* – focused on Queer country music and culture – not only introduced me to some of my best friends and most cherished chosen family, but also connected me to a sense of community and shared struggle and experience which has made what can seem like a lonely journey in the music industry feel like something I don't have to tackle alone.

Connecting with other marginalized musicians and allies all over the country is truly the reason I've been able to sustain my music career. Collaboration in the making of music itself has long been one of my greatest joys, but beyond that, building and being welcomed into community within an industry which can often feel quite cold and cutthroat, has sustained me through so much of my own disappointment and instances of imposter syndrome. Having folks with whom I'm able to share in triumphs and let- downs, as well as all of the highs and lows of life beyond music, has taught me so much about myself and the way I want to show up in the world. Seeing other queer artists and artists of color succeeding in music, and learning alongside them as independent musicians has changed the way I look at the music itself. No longer do I idealize the solitary, tortured artist, toiling away to "be discovered". Instead, I see community and collaboration as the bedrock of the music itself. Country and Americana music as we know them today, and even Pop and Rock and Roll, have evolved from The Blues, Gospel, Folk music, and the music of enslaved African people. The roots of American music run deep and they interconnect through origins of communal and familial music-making, long before musicians sang their songs in soundproof studios, in search of celebrity and fortune.

One evening, I was texting back and forth with Adeem, as we often do, when they jokingly said, "We're building a bonfire tonight. Wanna come over?" After chuckling, I was instantly hit in the chest with a pang of sadness at the realization that Adeem and their family live in Tennessee, while Andrés and I live almost 1,000 miles away in Massachusetts. This set off a chain reaction where Adeem and I both bemoaned the fact that we can't just drop in on one another from around the corner, wondering if we'll ever find ourselves living in the same city or state. I've had similar experiences with other chosen family who live about as far from me as Adeem, but I often find myself returning to an inexplicably warm feeling of deep gratitude at knowing that I have family all over the globe. The flip side of the loneliness of distance from loved ones is the realization that connection can span miles and even continents. What a joy it is for me to remember that there are folks in other states and time zones for whom

I hold so much love and who love me in return; to know that my bond with Jeannie has only grown stronger over shared memes, texts, and calls across the distance.

And what of my family of birth, whose intersecting stories have so deeply informed my own identity? In 2017, shortly after Andrés and I were married, he finished his doctorate and prepared to go on the job market in search of a tenure-track position in academia. I was terrified, having lived my entire adult life no more than an hour away from my parents and sisters, and here my spouse and I were, looking for an academic position in an incredibly difficult job market, wherever we might land.

As it turned out, both of our teaching positions brought us to Boston, 300 miles from Philadelphia, where I'd assumed I'd spend the rest of my life. Andrés' experience as an international student through college and grad school made him somewhat immune to the idea of "home" in a permanent sense. Now we were married, and I was home, he said. While I felt similarly in some respects, the codependency in which I'd been raised pulled strongly on my heart, and I wondered who I really was without my family close by.

The distance, while at times difficult, has been enlightening for me. We were always a family who got together for every holiday. We took summer vacations to the Jersey Shore together well into my and my sisters' adulthood, and it often pains me to see my nieces and nephew growing up from hundreds of miles away, often talking only through a computer screen. And yet, the distance has given me space to reckon with the traumas of my youth, and how my family's interconnectedness has perhaps stymied my own development of a sense of self. I've had to reckon with a great deal of repressed bitterness at the ways I've felt unseen as a trans person by my parents in the past, as well as the grief I've experienced at having so much of my childhood queerness "stolen" by religious dogma.

And yet, the physical space between myself and my parents and sisters has allowed me to step back and see them – truly see them in their complex, flawed, and beautiful wholeness – for the first time. Thanks in no small part to the work of my therapist, not only am I learning to see and love myself, but I'm also learning how to see my family as separate, fully autonomous, and beautifully flawed human beings; in a sense, we have never been closer.

I recently spent a week with my parents on the Delaware coast where they now live. For a few years, while I was still identifying as nonbinary and using they series pronouns, I dreaded any extended time spent with my mother in particular, as I expected that she would repeatedly misgender me and call me by my deadname. This went on for years, well beyond the "adjustment period" needed to get used to new language, and I often felt as though she just refused to see me. She wasn't malicious; ideologically she was accepting and affirming, and yet something felt as though it was missing in our own interactions with each other.

And yet, since this past February, when I began using she-series pronouns and undergoing HRT, something seemed to click into place. My mother has been almost gleeful at the prospect of having "another daughter," sharing makeup tips, and offering to let me go through her closet for clothes she no longer wears. It seems to me as though this has been a conscious effort on her part, perhaps to make up for the previous times I've come out to her and the ways she has responded in the past. In the lead up to this last visit, I found myself excited for the first time in years to spend time with her and my dad. When I was there, she took me to her part-time job at the local YMCA and relished in introducing me to her coworkers as her daughter. For the first time, I sat with my parents and spoke with them as fellow humans – just as scared and uncertain as I often am, and freed from the idealized expectations of a small child that her parents be infallible.

Writing this collection of stories and song lyrics has been an exercise in gratitude. In spite of the trauma I've mined in these pages, I always seem to come back to the idea that my queer story is not one of a lone heroine, with her face to the wind as she stands in epic struggle against the world. I was asked to write a text that would give personal perspective on the life of a queer, trans person living in the United States at the turn of the twenty-first century, and while I believe I've fulfilled the brief, I am reminded that I am a person blessed with the warm and loving embrace of my community – my chosen and birth families. This has been as much a story of the people who have walked alongside me as it is of mine.

Study questions

1. Discuss the role of friendship as a source of resilience in DeSilva's writings drawing from the framework of "chosen family" as originally explored by Kath Weston in *Families We Choose: Lesbians, Gays, Kinship* (1991) and since popularized in mainstream queer vernacular.

2.   Discuss the role of marriage in DeSilva's narrative using the framework of "homonormativity" as critiqued by Lisa Duggan in her 2002 essay "The New Homonormativity: The Sexual Politics of Neoliberalism."

References

Beautiful Thing (1996) Directed by Hettie MacDonald [DVD]. United Kingdom: FilmFour Distributors.

Connell, R.W. (1995). *Masculinities*. London: Routledge.

DeSilva, J. (2021). *Queen of the Backyard*. [song] Boston. Dirty Shoes Music.

DeSilva, J. (2023). *Sundays*. [song] Boston. Dirty Shoes Music.

DeSilva, J. (2023). *Firecracker*. [song] Boston. Dirty Shoes Music.

DeSilva, J. & Tasjan, A.L. (2024). *Glitter Up the Dark*. [song] Boston. Dirty Shoes Music.

DeSilva, J. & Calabrese, A. (2022). *The Devil in New Jersey*. [song] Boston. Dirty Shoes Music.

DeSilva, J. & Calabrese, A. (2022). *10,000 Things*. [song] Boston. Dirty Shoes Music.

DeSilva, J. & Calabrese, A. (2024). *Comrades in Arms*. [song] Boston. Dirty Shoes Music.

DeSilva, J., Woods, H. Woods G. (2020). *Family Tree*. [song] Boston. Dirty Shoes Music.

DeSilva, J. & Dunn, J. (2019). *Jeannie Frances*. [song] Boston. Dirty Shoes Music.

Doty, A. 1993. *Making things perfectly queer: Interpreting mass culture*. Minneapolis, MN: University of Minnesota Press.

Duggan, L. 2002. The new homonormativity: The sexual politics of neoliberalism. *Materializing democracy: Toward a revitalized cultural politics*, *10*, pp.175–194.

Marrs, T. 1989. *Ravaged by the new age: Satan's plan to destroy our kids*. Redmond, WA: Living Truth Publishers.

Muñoz, J.E. 2019. *Cruising utopia: The then and there of queer futurity*. New York: New York University Press.

Pascoe, C.J. 2007. *Dude, you're a fag: Masculinity and sexuality in high school*. Berkeley, CA: University of California Press.

Stockton, K.B. 2009. *The queer child, or growing sideways in the twentieth century*. Durham, NC: Duke University Press.

Weston, K. 1991. *Families we choose: Lesbians, gays, kinship*. New York: Columbia University Press.

Index

www.ingramcontent.com/pod-product-compliance
Lightning Source LLC
Chambersburg PA
CBHW070350270326
41926CB00017B/4070